Babylon.js Essentials

Understand, train, and be ready to develop 3D Web
applications/video games using the Babylon.js framework,
even for beginners

Julien Moreau-Mathis

BIRMINGHAM - MUMBAI

Babylon.js Essentials

Publishing Month: February 2016

Production reference: 1230216

Published by Packt Publishing Ltd.
Livery Place
35 Livery Street
Birmingham
B3 2PB, UK.
ISBN 978-1-78588-479-5

www.packtpub.com

Credits

About the Author

Julien Moreau-Mathis is a fan of 3D development. He started working with 3D development at the age of 17 and created a C++ framework named Community Play 3D. Now, he is a developer at Microsoft and he takes immense pleasure in being a part of the Babylon.js team.

About the Reviewer

Sergio Martínez-Losa del Rincón lives in Spain. He is a software engineer and entrepreneur.

He has always enjoyed writing technical documents as well as programming in several languages. He is always keen on learning new programming languages and facing new challenges. He has been creating applications and games for iPhone, Macintosh, Android, Google Glass, Unity3D, and Cocos2d-x. Sergio likes VR technologies and all kinds of challenges. He also likes web programming and designing good APIs for mobile applications.

So far, Sergio has developed all kinds of applications in Java, C++, Objective-C, PHP, and various other languages. He is now developing products in the IoT field using SaaS technologies. Sergio likes to explore cloud services in order to expand the application possibilities, he also likes machine learning technologies and natural language processing to study new ways of using big data.

You can see a part of his work here at `http://goo.gl/k5tOSX`.

www.PacktPub.com

For support files and downloads related to your book, please visit www.PacktPub.com .

Did you know that Packt offers eBook versions of every book published, with PDF and ePub files available? You can upgrade to the eBook version at www.PacktPub.com and as a print book customer, you are entitled to a discount on the eBook copy. Get in touch with us at service@packtpub.com for more details.

At www.PacktPub.com , you can also read a collection of free technical articles, sign up for a range of free newsletters and receive exclusive discounts and offers on Packt books and eBooks.

https://www2.packtpub.com/books/subscription/packtlib

Do you need instant solutions to your IT questions? PacktLib is Packt's online digital book library. Here, you can search, access, and read Packt's entire library of books.

Why subscribe?

- Fully searchable across every book published by Packt
- Copy and paste, print, and bookmark content
- On demand and accessible via a web browser

Free access for Packt account holders

If you have an account with Packt at www.PacktPub.com, you can use this to access PacktLib today and view 9 entirely free books. Simply use your login credentials for immediate access.

Table of Contents

Preface

3D development has always been something mystic. Starting from the beginning, this book introduces the required basics of 3D development and the knowledge you require to use the Babylon.js framework. It focuses on the simplicity provided by Babylon.js and uses a combination of theory and practice. All the chapters are provided with example files that are ready to run; each example file provides the previously learned features of the framework. Finally, the developers will be ready to easily understand the new features that are added to the framework in the future and use the more advanced features only using the documentation.

What this book covers

Chapter 1, *Babylon.js and the TypeScript Language*, provides a quick introduction to the Babylon.js story and a course on a fundamental that is the TypeScript language.

Chapter 2, *The Fundamentals of Babylon.js and Available Tools*, starts with the Babylon.js framework and creates the first 3D scene, showing the simplicity of the framework along with the theory.

Chapter 3, *Create, Load, and Draw 3D Objects on the Screen*, starts with the concepts of Chapter 2, *The Fundamentals of Babylon.js and Available Tools*, let's introduce the right way to create 3D scenes and work with 3D artists.

Chapter 4, *Using Materials to Customize 3D Objects Appearance*, explains the notion of materials in 3D engines. In other words, let's unleash the Babylon.js Standard Material.

Chapter 5, *Create Collisions on Objects*, focuses on the gameplay itself by managing the collisions in your scenes, including physics simulation.

Chapter 6, *Manage Audio in Babylon.js*, explains one of the added values of the Babylon.js framework. Let's add and manage sounds, including spatialized sounds, in your scenes.

Chapter 7, *Defining Actions on Objects*, introduces a smart way to trigger actions on the 3D objects themselves without to many lines of code as some tasks can be a pain for developers.

Chapter 8, *Add Rendering Effects Using Built-in Post-processes*, shows the preferred part of most of the 3D developers. This shows and explains how to easily beautify the 3D scenes using post-processes effects, combined with the simplicity provided by Babylon.js.

Chapter 9, *Create and Play Animations*, allows us to play with the animations system provided by Babylon.js. This chapter provides the final skill that you need in order to be ready to build your own professional 3D application!

What you need for this book

This book targets HTML5 developers, who want to build complete 3D video games or applications on browsers. The reader should have some familiarity with the JavaScript language and basic 3D representations (notion of vectors and dimensions). The Babylon.js framework is designed to be easy to use, therefore, no 3D development background is needed and beginners are welcome.

Who this book is for

Babylon.js Essentials is intended for developers, who want to enter the world of 3D development for the Web or add the Babylon.js framework to their skill set. The notion of object-oriented programming would be helpful to understand the architecture of the Babylon.js framework. Also, familiarity with Web development would be useful to understand the principles used.

Conventions

In this book, you will find a number of text styles that distinguish between different kinds of information. Here are some examples of these styles and an explanation of their meaning. Code words in text, database table names, folder names, filenames, file extensions, pathnames, dummy URLs, user input, and Twitter handles are shown as follows: "With TS, typing new `Array()` is equivalent to new `Array<any>()`."

A block of code is set as follows:

```
var skybox = BABYLON.Mesh.CreateBox("skybox", 300, scene);
var skyboxMaterial = new BABYLON.StandardMaterial("skyboxMaterial", scene);
skyboxMaterial.backFaceCulling = false;
skyboxMaterial.reflectionTexture =
  new BABYLON.CubeTexture("skybox/TropicalSunnyDay", scene);
```

Any command-line input or output is written as follows:

```
var myVar: FileAccess = FileAccess.Read; // Equivalent to 0
```

New terms and important words are shown in bold. Words that you see on the screen, for example, in menus or dialog boxes, appear in the text like this: "Select the file location as you did for Blender to save the Babylon.js scene and click on **Export**."

Warnings or important notes appear in a box like this.

Tips and tricks appear like this.

Reader feedback

Feedback from our readers is always welcome. Let us know what you think about this book-what you liked or disliked. Reader feedback is important for us as it helps us develop titles that you will really get the most out of.

To send us general feedback, simply e-mail feedback@packtpub.com, and mention the book's title in the subject of your message.

If there is a topic that you have expertise in and you are interested in either writing or contributing to a book, see our author guide at www.packtpub.com/authors.

Customer support

Now that you are the proud owner of a Packt book, we have a number of things to help you to get the most from your purchase.

Downloading the example code

You can download the example code files from your account at http://www.packtpub.com for all the Packt Publishing books you have purchased. If you purchased this book elsewhere, you can visit http://www.packtpub.com/support and register to have the files e-mailed directly to you.

Downloading the color images of this book

We also provide you with a PDF file that has color images of the screenshots/diagrams used in this book. The color images will help you better understand the changes in the output. You can download this file from `https://www.packtpub.com/sites/default/files/downloads/BabylonJSEssentials_ColorImages.pdf`.

Errata

Although we have taken every care to ensure the accuracy of our content, mistakes do happen. If you find a mistake in one of our books-maybe a mistake in the text or the code-we would be grateful if you could report this to us. By doing so, you can save other readers from frustration and help us improve subsequent versions of this book. If you find any errata, please report them by visiting `http://www.packtpub.com/submit-errata`, selecting your book, clicking on the **Errata Submission Form** link, and entering the details of your errata. Once your errata are verified, your submission will be accepted and the errata will be uploaded to our website or added to any list of existing errata under the Errata section of that title.

To view the previously submitted errata, go to `https://www.packtpub.com/books/content/support` and enter the name of the book in the search field. The required information will appear under the `Errata` section.

Piracy

Piracy of copyrighted material on the Internet is an ongoing problem across all media. At Packt, we take the protection of our copyright and licenses very seriously. If you come across any illegal copies of our works in any form on the Internet, please provide us with the location address or website name immediately so that we can pursue a remedy.

Please contact us at `copyright@packtpub.com` with a link to the suspected pirated material.

We appreciate your help in protecting our authors and our ability to bring you valuable content.

Questions

If you have a problem with any aspect of this book, you can contact us at `questions@packtpub.com`, and we will do our best to address the problem.

Babylon.js and the TypeScript Language

Babylon.js is a framework that allows you to create complete 3D applications and 3D video games for the Web. Babylon.js has a community that grows day after day; a community that actively contributes to the project, adding more and more features. This chapter gives you a brief introduction to the framework's vision and the TypeScript language as, Babylon.js was developed using this.

The Babylon.js framework embeds all the necessary tools to handle specific 3D applications. It allows you to load and draw 3D objects, manage these 3D objects, create and manage special effects, play and manage spatialized sounds, create gameplays, and more. Babylon.js is an easy-to-use framework as you can set up (you'll see this later) these things with the minimum lines of code.

Babylon.js is a JavaScript framework developed using TypeScript. TypeScript is a compiled and multiplatform language that generates pure JavaScript files.

We will cover the following topics in this chapter:

- An introduction to Babylon.js
- The reason Babylon.js has been developed using TypeScript
- An introduction to TypeScript

The creators

Babylon.js was created by David Catuhe (@deltakosh), David Rousset (@davrous), Pierre Lagarde (@pierlag), and Michel Rousseau (@rousseau_michel). It's an open source project essentially developed in their spare time. When they started Babylon.js, they wanted it to be designed as *easy-to-use* and then get an accessible 3D engine for everyone. The official web site (http://www.babylonjs.com/) contains a lot of tutorials for beginners (even in 3D) to more advanced users with examples for each feature and scenes as examples.

Online tools provided by the Babylon.js solution

Babylon.js provides you with several online tools to help developers and artists experiment and try their productions:

- For developers, the Playground (http://www.babylonjs-playground.com/) allows you to experiment and train. It shows a code editor with autocompletion (Monaco) and canvas to see the results. It also provides some examples of code to train with.
- For artists, the Sandbox (http://www.babylonjs.com/sandbox/) allows you to drag and drop exported Babylon.js scenes (Blender and 3ds Max) to the browser to see the results in real time. The Sandbox provides you with debugging tools to activate/deactivate features and see the impact on real-time performances.
- The **CreateYour Own Shader** (**CYOS**) allows developers to develop shaders and see the results in real time. There are also several shaders already available to train and experiment with.

Why is Babylon.js developed using TypeScript?

Babylon.js is a big project with increasing contributions since its creation on GitHub. It provides you with a lot of functions and, sometimes, with a lot of parameters for more flexibility. The TypeScript language is useful for robust code as its goal is to improve and secure the production of JavaScript code.

The TypeScript language

TypeScript (**TS**) is a free and open source language developed by Microsoft. It is a compiled language to produce JavaScript (the TS code is, in fact, transcompiled) and provides a static typing system, which is optional. The typing system is used in Babylon.js in order to get a cleaner and more descriptive code. It means that if a function has a lot of parameters, it's easier to fill and understand them instead of always using the documentation as a reference. Moreover, it allows developers to declare classes (as the ECMAScript 6 specifications do) and interfaces for a better understandable architecture and structure of code.

The TypeScript features

The typing system is powerful as it allows developers to create interfaces, enumerated types, and classes and handle generics and union typing. Overall, developers use the typing system for a better understanding and security of the libraries that they are building and using.

The TS language supports inheritance (classes) and also provides access specifiers (private / public / protected) to modify the access rights for the classes' members. Then, developers can see at a glance the members that they can use and modify.

Introduction to TypeScript – what you have to know

Let's introduce TypeScript with some feature examples and configurations: how to compile TS files to JS files, work with classes / types / union types, functions, inheritance, and interfaces.

Compilation using Gulp

Gulp is a task runner available as an npm package. It provides a plugin to handle the TypeScript compilation. The only thing to do is to configure a task using gulp with gulp-typescript.

To download the gulp packages, you have to install Node.js (https://nodejs.org/) to get access to the npm packages:

1. Install Gulp using the following command line:

   npm install gulp

2. Install Gulp-Typescript using the following command lines:

   npm install gulp-typescript

3. To configure the Gulp task, just provide a JS file named `gulpfile.js` containing the task description.

4. Import Gulp and Gulp-TypeScript:

```
var gulp = require("gulp");
var ts = require("gulp-typescript");
```

5. Define the default task to transcompile your TS files:

```
gulp.task('default', function() { // Default task
  var result = gulp.src([ // Sources
      "myScript1.ts",
      "myScript2.ts",
      // Other files here
    ])
    .pipe(ts({ // Trans-compile
      out: "outputFile.js" // Merge into one output file
    }));
  return result.js.pipe(gulp.dest("./")); // output file desti
  nation
});
```

6. Once the default task lists all the TS files to transcompile, just call Gulp using the following command line:

```
gulp
```

Working with typed variables

Working with TypeScript is really similar to JS as the typing system is optional. Nevertheless, the common types in TS are as follows:

- String
- Number
- Boolean
- Any
- Void
- Enum
- Array

With JS, you should write the following:

```
var myVar = 1.0;// or
```

```
var myVar = "hello !";
```

Here, you can write exactly the same with TS. The TS compiler will process the type inference and guess the variable type for you:

```
var myVar = 1.0; // Which is a number
// or
var myVar = "hello !"; // Which is a string
```

To specify the type of a variable with TS, type the following command:

```
var myVar: type = value;
```

Then, with the previous example, add the following code:

```
var myVar: number = 1.0;
// or
var myVar: string = "hello !";
// etc.
```

However, it's forbidden to assign a new value with a different type even if you don't mention the type as follows:

```
var myVar = 1.0; // Now, myVar is a number
// and
myVar = "hello !"; // Forbidden, "hello" is a string and not a number
```

To get the JS flexibility with variables, let's introduce the any type. The any type allows developers to create variables without any static type. The following is an example:

```
var myVar: any = 1.0; // Is a number but can be anything else
myVar = "Hello !"; // Allowed, myVar's type is "any"
```

The following is the screenshot of the types.ts file:

```
types.ts
1 this.trainWithTypes = () => {
2     var notSpecified = 1.0;
3     var specified: number = 1.0;
4     var anySpecified: any = 1.0;
5
6     notSpecified = "Hello !";
7     anySpecified = "Hello !";
8 };
9
```

Let's introduce some specific types. It's the occasion to introduce the generics using

TypeScript and enumerated types. The usage of numbers, Booleans, and strings is the same in TypeScript and JavaScript. So, no need to learn more.

Enumerated types

Working withenumerated types (enum) is like working with numbers. The syntax is as follows:

```
enum FileAccess {Read, Write};
```

This generates the following JS code:

```
var FileAccess;
(function (FileAccess) {
    FileAccess[FileAccess["Read"] = 0] = "Read";
    FileAccess[FileAccess["Writer"] = 1] = "Writer";
})(FileAccess || (FileAccess = {}));
```

Access to an enumerated type in both the languages is as follows:

```
var myVar: FileAccess = FileAccess.Read; // Equivalent to 0
```

Array

Defining an array with TS is also similar to JS. The following is an example:

```
// In both languages
var myArray = [];
// or
var myArray = new Array();
```

With TS, array is a generic class. Then, you can specify the item's type contained in the array as follows:

```
var myArray = new Array<number>();
```

 Note: With TS, typing new `Array()` is equivalent to new `Array<any>()`.

You can now access the common functions as follows:

```
var myArray = new Array<any>();
myArray.push("Hello !");
```

```
myArray.push("1");
myArray.splice(0, 1);
console.log(myArray); // "[1]"
```

Working with classes and interfaces

Classes and interfaces allow you to build types just as the `Array` class does. Once you create a class, you can create instances using the keyword `new`, which creates an object in the memory.

The following is an example:

```
var myArray = new Array<any>(); // Creates a new instance
```

Creating a class

The syntax in TS to define a class is as follows:

```
class Writer {
  constructor() {
    // initialize some things here
  }
}
```

This generates the following in JS:

```
var Writer = (function () {
    function Writer() {
    }
    return Writer;
})();
```

In both languages, you can create an instance of `Writer`:

```
var myInstance = new Writer();
```

You can also use modules that work as namespaces:

```
module MY_MODULE {
  class Writer {
    ...
  }
}
```

Access:

```
var writer = new MY_MODULE.Writer(...);
```

Creating class members

With JS and the conventions, you can write the following:

```
function Writer() {
  this.myPublicMember = 0.0; // A public member
  this._myPrivateMember = 1.0; // A member used as private
}
```

With TS, you can explicitly specify the access specifier of a member (public, private, and protected), which has been explained as follows:

- **Public**: Any block of code can access the member to read and write
- **Private**: Only this can access this member to read and write
- **Protected**: External blocks of code cannot access the member; only this and specializers (inheritance) can access this member to read and write

Let's experiment using the Writer class:

```
// declare class
class Writer {
  // Union types. Can be a "string" or
// an array of strings "Array<string>"
  public message: string|string[];
  private _privateMessage: string = "private message";
  protected _protectedMessage: string;

  // Constructor. Called by the "new" keyword
  constructor(message: string|string[]) {
    this.message = message;
    this._protectedMessage = "Protected message !"; // Allowed
}

// A public function accessible from everywhere.
// Returns nothing. Then, its return type is "void".
public write(): void {
  console.log(this.message); // Allowed
  console.log(this._privateMessage); // Allowed
  console.log(this._protectedMessage); // Allowed
}
}

var writer = new Writer("My Public Message !");
console.log(writer.message); // Allowed
```

```
console.log(writer._privateMessage); // Not allowed
console.log(writer._protectedMessage); // Not allowed
```

Working with inheritance

Let's create a new class that specializes the `Writer` class. The specialized classes can access all the public and protected members of the base class thanks to the inheritance. The `extends` keyword represents the inheritance.

Let's create a new class named `BetterWriter` that specializes (extends) the `Writer` class:

```
// The base class is "Writer"
class BetterWriter extends Writer {
  constructor(message: string|string[]) {
    // Call the base class' constructor
    super(message);
}

// We can override the "write" function
public write(): void {
  if (typeof this.message === "string") {
    // Call the function "write" of the base class
    // which is the "Writer" class
    super.write();
  }
  else {
    for (var i=0; i < this.message.length; i++) {
      console.log(this.message[i]); // Allowed
      console.log(this._privateMessage); // Not allowed
      console.log(this._protectedMessage); // Allowed
    }
  }
}
}
```

Using interfaces

Interfaces are used to create contracts. It means that if a class implements an interface, the class must provide all the functions and members defined in the interface. If not, it doesn't respect the contract, and the compiler will output an error.

All the defined functions are public and all the defined members are public.

With Babylon.js, a good example is to use the `IDisposable` interface. It means that the users can call the method named `dispose()`. This function's job is to deactivate and/or deallocate the systems used.

The following is an example:

```
interface IWriter {
  // The class "Writer" must have the "message" member
  message: string|string[];
  // The class "Writer" must provide the "resetMessages" function.
  resetMessages(): void;
}

class Writer implements IWriter {
  public message: string|string[];
  ...
  constructor(...) {
    ...
  }
  ...
  // All functions declared in the interface are public.
  public resetMessages(): void {
    this.message = this._privateMessage = this._protectedMessage = "";
  }
}
```

Summary

In this chapter, you obtained the necessary knowledge to develop programs using TypeScript with Babylon.js. You'll see that working with TypeScript can be more productive and secure in most cases. Additionally, some developers will be more comfortable when using types as they are used to development with typing.

Don't hesitate to manipulate TypeScript with the attached example files. Don't forget to install gulp and run the command lines.

You can also run the following command line:

```
gulp watch
```

This will track and recompile the TS files at each modification automatically.

In the next chapter, let's get straight to the heart of the matter with an introduction to the Babylon.js framework, and how to create an engine and scene entities such as lights, cameras, and meshes (3D objects). You'll build your first 3D scene with Babylon.js and understand the architecture of the framework really quickly!

2
The Fundamentals of Babylon.js and Available Tools

This chapter presents the fundamentals of Babylon.js. It includes the notions of *engine*, *scene*, *camera*, *light*, *mesh*, and so on. By practicing, you'll understand the basic tools used in 3D such as vectors and how/where they are used in 3D engines. You'll also practice with graph structures and understand the architecture of Babylon.js.

The following topics will be covered in this chapter:

- Discussing the Babylon.js structure and graphs
- Creating your first scene

The Babylon.js structure and graphs

First, let's create and explain the necessary tools to draw things on the screen, such as an engine that will handle a scene to draw a 3D object and use a camera and light.

The engine and a scene

The engine is the core of Babylon.js and a scene allows you to create and manage entities that you'll draw on the screen (objects, lights, cameras, and so on), thanks to an engine. You can see the engine like a gateway to communicate with the video card (GPU) while a scene is a high-level interface that handles the following multiple entities:

- 3D objects (more on this in `Chapter 3`, *Create, Load, and Draw 3D Objects on the Screen*)

- Cameras
- Lights
- Particle systems (smoke, rain, and others)
- Textures
- Skeletons (animated 3D objects)
- Post-processes (effects)
- Materials (more on this in Chapter 4, *Using Materials to Customize 3D Objects Appearance*)
- Sprites

In other words, a scene handles multiple entities and will call the engine to draw these entities on the screen.

To draw on the screen, the web page (index.html) must contain a canvas. The canvas is used to create the WebGL context that the engine will use. The only parameter needed to create an engine is the canvas and the only parameter needed to create a scene is an engine.

The canvas in the web page is as follows:

```
<canvas id="renderCanvas"></canvas>
```

The following code is performed to render on the entire page:

```
<style>
    html, body {
        overflow: hidden;
        width: 100%;
        height: 100%;
        margin: 0;
        padding: 0;
    }

    #renderCanvas {
        width: 100%;
        height: 100%;
    }
</style>
```

To create an engine, you have to give the canvas reference as a parameter. Get the reference of the DOM object as follows:

```
var canvas = document.getElementById("renderCanvas");
```

Create an engine by passing the canvas reference:

```
var engine: BABYLON.Engine = new BABYLON.Engine(canvas);
```

Create a scene as follows:

```
var scene: BABYLON.Scene = new BABYLON.Scene(engine);
```

Each new scene created is stored in `engine.scenes`, which is an array of `BABYLON.Scene`.

Once you create a scene, you can render every frame (60 frames per second in a perfect case and less if your hardware isn't sufficient). To perform this action, you have to call the `engine.runRunderLoop(function)` function. The anonymous function `function` is called every frame and this is the place to draw the scene:

```
// runRenderLoop with TypeScript. The anonymous function doesn't
// have any parameter
engine.runRenderLoop(() => {
    scene.render();
});
```

The `scene.render()` function is called to draw every object on the screen during the frame.

Adding cameras and lights

Once you create a scene, you can create objects such as lights and cameras. The minimal scene requirement is composed of a camera (needed to get a view in the scene) and light (that illuminates the 3D objects in the scene, but this is not required if objects in the scene are self-illuminated).

Adding a camera

There are several types of cameras and lights. The Babylon.js framework provides you with a fixed camera (no movements), FPS camera, rotation camera (turns around a point), gamepad camera (XBOX 360 gamepad), and touch camera (for touch devices). All these cameras can be created in the scene with a minimum number of lines of code. For example, let's start with a free camera (FPS) with its position at coordinates (x=10,y=20,z=30). This is the occasion to introduce the `BABYLON.Vector3` class:

```
var camera =  new BABYLON.FreeCamera("cameraName", new BABYLON.Vector3(10,
20, 30), scene);
```

The constructor needs a name (`cameraName`), position for the camera, and scene reference (where to add the camera). The position is in the `BABYLON.Vector3(x, y, z)` type, which is the 3D vector class of Babylon.js. The `Vector3` object provides mathematical functions such as addition, subtraction, multiplication, division, and more.

Once you create the camera, let's change the camera's position and perform a `Vector3` addition:

```
camera.position = new BABYLON.Vector3(10, 0, 10).addInPlace(new
BABYLON.Vector3(0, 10, 0));
```

The `.addInPlace` method modifies the current instance of `Vector3`, but you can also call the `.add` method that will return a new instance of `Vector3` with the addition applied.

The new position of the camera is now (x=10,y=10,z=10). Modifying the `.position` property does not work for all the cameras, especially the rotation camera (`BABYLON.ArcRotateCamera`). The rotation camera turns around a point (which is the target of the camera) and can be explained as follows:

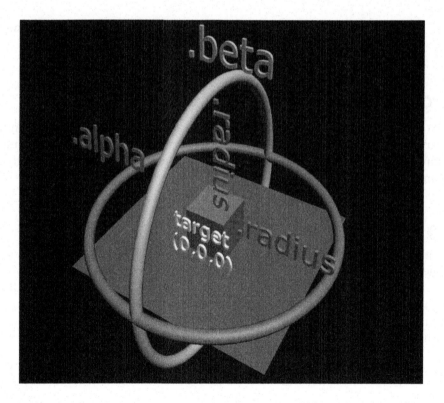

The cube is at the position (x=0,y=0,z=0) and is the target of the camera. To change the camera's position, you have to call the `camera.setPosition(position)` function. This function will calculate the appropriate values for the alpha (angle around Y), beta (angle around X), and radius. Then, the .position property is only left to read.

Adding a light

Once you create your camera, let's add a light. The different lights allow you to perform lighting in your scene with different features. The point lights and hemispheric lights tend to illuminate the objects in the scene, while the spot lights and directional lights also provide support for the real-time shadows.

Let's start with a point light. Lights work like cameras, which means that you have to provide the scene reference (where to add the light):

```
var light = new BABYLON.PointLight("lightName", BABYLON.Vector3.Zero(),
scene);
```

The second parameter is the light position. BABYLON.Vector3.Zero() is a static method that is a shortcut to create a Vector3 instance with coordinates (x=0,y=0,z=0). Now, let's play with the light's parameters:

```
light.position = new BABYLON.Vector3(20, 20, 20);
light.diffuse = new BABYLON.Color3(0, 1, 0);
light.specular = new BABYLON.Color3(1, 0, 0);
light.intensity = 1.0;
```

The following are the parameters of the preceding code:

- The .diffuse parameter represents the native color of the light, which is green in the example
- The .specular parameter represents the light color reflected by a surface, which is red here
- The .intensity parameter is the light's intensity that is equal to 1.0 by default

The following is the result of these parameters applied to a 3D object:

The following is achieved by modifying the specular color to red and blue:

Adding a mesh

What are meshes? In fact, 3D objects are what we call meshes. Their structure is pretty simple as they have two important buffers in memory:

- The vertex buffer is an array of 3D points: the vertices. The vertices represent the 3D points needed to build geometrical forms such as cubes, spheres, characters, weapons, and so on. For example, a cube has eight vertices.
- The index buffer, which is an array of numbers, represents the indices in the vertex buffer to build triangles. Indeed, graphic cards are optimized to calculate and render triangles on the screen. For example, a face of a cube will be rendered using two triangles, as shown in the following image, where the green lines show the face:

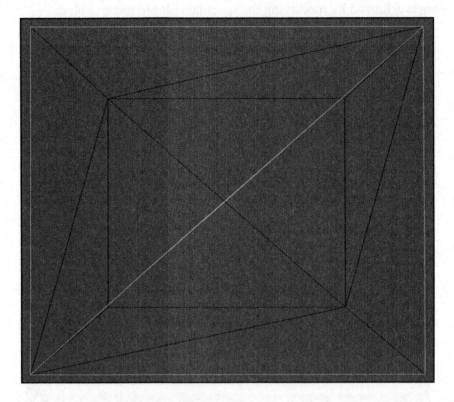

The job of graphic cards is separated into two steps:

- They project (transformation) the vertices (3D points) of the vertex buffer on the screen. These operations are performed by a GPU program named vertex shader. In other words, the vertex shader computes the 2D position of each triangle.
- They fill the pixels associated with the triangles with their colors using a GPU program named pixel shader.

To conclude the graphic cards' job, the vertex shader computes the 2D triangles on the screen and the pixel shader illuminates the pixels with different colors.

Using Babylon.js to create meshes

Babylon.js provides you with static methods in the BABYLON.Mesh class that allow you to create basic meshes such as boxes, spheres, and torus. Every created mesh is an instance of BABYLON.Mesh. Let's start with a box:

```
var box = BABYLON.Mesh.CreateBox("boxName", size, scene);
```

The `size` parameter represents the distance between the vertices (for example, 5) and the `scene` parameter is the scene reference (where to add the mesh). Once you get the mesh created, you can access its properties and methods as follows:

```
box.position = new BABYLON.Vector3(0, 2.5, 0);
box.rotation = new BABYLON.Vector3(0, Math.PI / 4, 0);
box.scaling = new BABYLON.Vector3(2, 2, 2);
```

The `.rotation` parameter represents the mesh's rotation expressed in radians `[0, 2π]`, and then, in degrees, `π = 180 degrees` and `2π = 360 degrees`.

The `.scaling` parameter represents the mesh's scale in three directions (*x,y,z*). In the example, the mesh is two times bigger.

Let's see the result if you modify its rotation only:

The following image is the result of applying a new scale, (x=2,y=2,z=2):

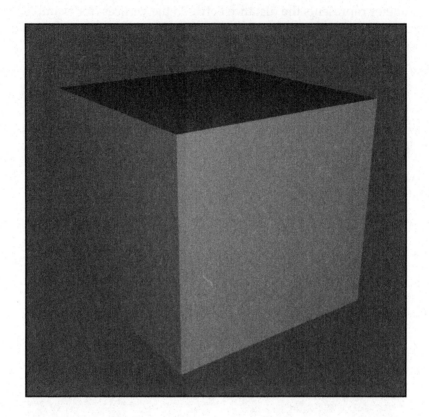

Some other basic meshes

There exist multiple basic meshes that `BABYLON.Mesh` can create for you, such as spheres and planes. Let's create a sphere and plane using the `BABYLON.Mesh` class:

```
var sphere = BABYLON.Mesh.CreateSphere("sphereName", segments, size,
scene);
var plane = BABYLON.Mesh.CreatePlane("planeName", size, scene);
```

The sphere's `segments` parameter represents the level of detail for the sphere, for example, 10.

The plane's `size` parameter represents the distance between vertices, for example, 10.

Managing a scene graph

The scene can be managed using a graph of nodes named scene graph. In Babylon.js, each mesh, light, and camera extends the `BABYLON.Node` class. In other words, each `BABYLON.Node` is in the scene graph.

Each node has an array of children and one, and only one, parent. Each created node is a child of the graph's root by default.

To modify the parent of a node, just modify the node's reference:

```
light.parent = camera;
```

Now, because the light is a child of the camera, the light's position depends on the camera's position. Indeed, the light space is a subspace of the camera. In other words, you can see the position (x=0,y=0,z=0) as the position of the camera.

When setting a parent, the transformation properties (position, rotation, and scaling) of the children are influenced by the parent.

An example

Let's manage the scene graph with two nodes (`node1` and `node2`) and compare it with the equivalent code if you were to do it manually:

```
node1.position = new BABYLON.Vector3(0, 0, 0);
node1.parent = node2;
```

This is equivalent to the following code:

```
engine.runRenderLoop(() => {
  node1.position = node2.position;
  node1.rotation = node2.rotation;
  node1.scaling = node2.scaling;
});
```

The following schema explains the preceding code:

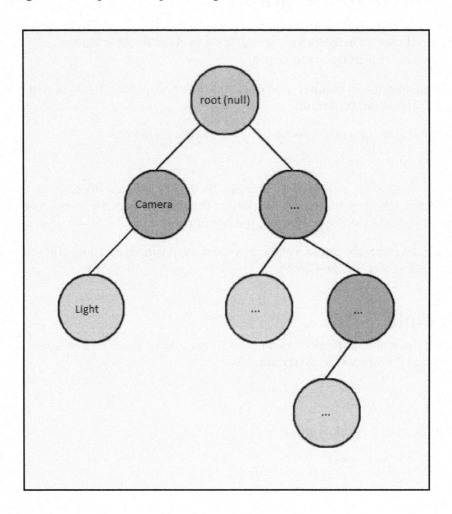

Creating your first scene

Now, you have all the necessary elements to build your first scene. Here, the scene will be composed of a rotation camera, point light, and box. Let's create a class using TypeScript and practice with Babylon.js.

Creating a class and the scene nodes

The following class creates the Babylon.js elements directly in the constructor:

```
export class BasicScene {
  public camera: BABYLON.ArcRotateCamera; // Our camera
  public light: BABYLON.PointLight; // Our light
  public box: BABYLON.Mesh; // Our box

  private _engine: BABYLON.Engine; // The Babylon.js engine
  private _scene: BABYLON.Scene; // The scene where to add the nodes

  // Our constructor. The constructor provides the canvas reference
  // Then, we can create the Babylon.js engine
  constructor(canvas: HTMLCanvasElement) {
    // Create engine
    this._engine = new BABYLON.Engine(canvas);

    // Create the scene
    this._scene = new BABYLON.Scene(this._engine);

    // Create the camera
    this.camera = new BABYLON.ArcRotateCamera("camera", 0, 0, 30,
BABYLON.Vector3.Zero(),
        this._scene);
    this.camera.attachControl(canvas, true);

    // Create the light
    this.light = new BABYLON.PointLight("light",new BABYLON.Vector3(20, 20,
20),
        this._scene);
    this.light.diffuse = new BABYLON.Color3(0, 1, 0);
this.light.specular = new BABYLON.Color3(1, 0, 1);
this.light.intensity = 1.0;

// Create the box
this.box = BABYLON.Mesh.CreateBox("cube", 5, this._scene);
  }
}
```

Call the runRenderLoop method

Let's add a method to the class that will call the `runRenderLoop` method:

```
public runRenderLoop(): void {
  this._engine.runRenderLoop(() => {
```

```
      this._scene.render();
    });
  }
```

This scene is exactly the same as mentioned in the previous image — there is a box and green light.

Managing the scene graph

To practice with the scene graph, let's create a method that will set the light as a child of the camera. The method will set the light's position at coordinates (x=0,y=0,z=0) and set the parent of the light as the camera:

```
public setCameraParentOfLight(): void {
  this.light.parent = this.camera;
}
```

Summary

In this chapter, you learned how to create a minimal HTML page to handle a Babylon.js engine and draw a scene. You also learned how to use Babylon.js' built-in nodes such as lights, cameras, and meshes.

Don't hesitate to practice with the built-in meshes such as torus, torus-knots, and spheres and play with the scene graph and node's properties such as position.

In the next chapter, you'll learn how scenes are built with designers and how they are imported using Babylon.js. You'll also see that interfacing 3D software to create scenes with Babylon.js is pretty easy as all the tools are provided by the Babylon.js solution (such as exporters and importers).

The next chapter will also explain how artists work to create 3D scenes for the web as their problems are different from desktop software such as games for consoles and PCs.

3

Create, Load, and Draw 3D Objects on the Screen

In the last chapter, you learned that 3D objects, called meshes, are composed of a list of 3D points (vertex buffer) and indices (index buffer) that creates the triangles that are drawn on the screen. To create complex meshes such as characters or buildings, 3D artists use modeling software that is capable of handling the vertex buffers and index buffers for us, including a lot of powerful tools for an easy creation.

The Babylon.js solution comes with plugins for Blender (https://www.blender.org/) and 3ds Max (http://www.autodesk.fr/products/3ds-max/overview), two famous modelers known by artists. These plugins are intended for 3D artists and are used to export the scenes built in these modelers to a format that Babylon.js is capable of loading. The exported files are JSON files with the .babylon extension. More information about the format can be found at http://doc.babylonjs.com/generals/File_Format_Map_(.babylon).

In this chapter, we will cover the following topics:

- Using Blender to export scenes
- Using 3ds Max to export scenes
- Loading scenes with Babylon.js programmatically

Using Blender to export scenes

Blender is a free and open source modeler to create 3D models using specialized tools. Blender is famous as it is cross-platform (works on Windows, Mac OS X, and Linux) and is known as a better 3D modeler in the world of open source (powerful tools for 3D rendering, animations, texturing, and so on). For more information about its features and demos, you can visit `https://www.blender.org`.

Moreover, Blender allows developers to create plugins written with the Python language, a feature that allowed the Babylon.js team to develop the Blender's exporter. In fact, the Babylon.js exporter will allow you to build your scenes (including meshes, lights, cameras, and so on) directly in Blender and easily export your scenes to a Babylon.js format that you'll be able to load in your projects. Let's take a look at the following steps and see how you can (still easily) do this.

Setting up the Babylon.js exporter for Blender

In the Babylon.js GitHub repository, you'll find a folder containing the Blender plugin in `Exporters/Blender/`. The `io_scene_map` folder and the `io_export_babylon.py` file are to be copied to the `addons` folder of Blender (typically located at `C:\Program Files\Blender Foundation\2.75\scripts\addons\`):

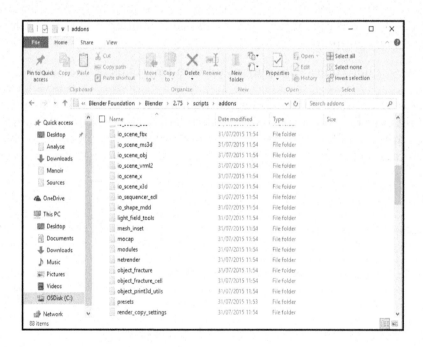

Once the files are copied, just activate the plugin so that it appears in the exporter's menu. The result, after activation, will look as follows:

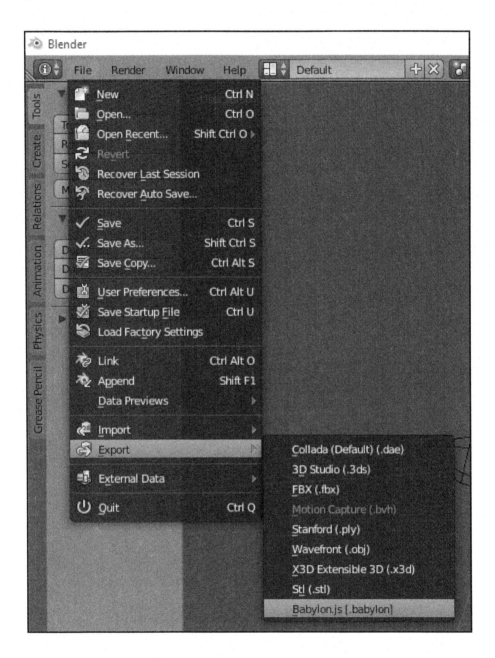

Activating the Babylon.js exporter in Blender

To activate the plugin, follow this procedure:

    1. Go to **User Preferences...**:

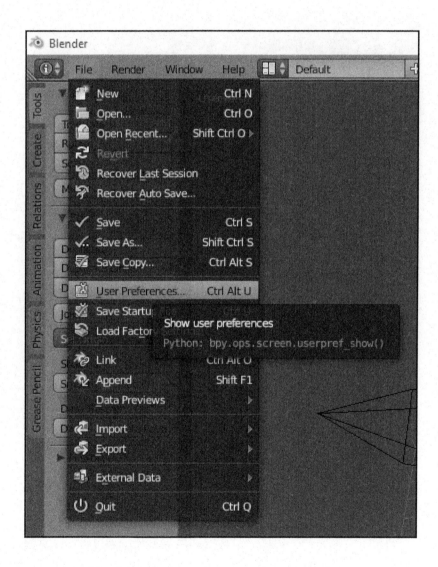

    1. Click on the **Add-ons** tab.

    2. Search for `babylon` in the search bar.

3. Activate the plugin.
4. Save the user settings:

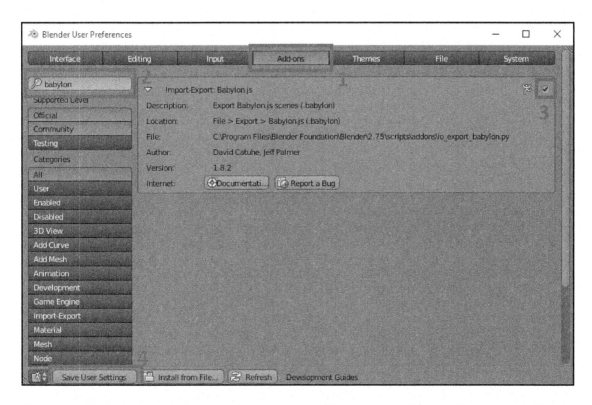

Once the plugin is activated, the plugin appears in the exporters' menu. You are now able to export scenes for Babylon.js.

Exporting a scene

Let's start with the initial scene created by default: a cube, camera, and light. Right-click on the cube to select it. Now, let's take a look at the properties on the right-hand side. (Refer to the following screenshots.) Thanks to the plugin, there is a specific zone for Babylon.js. These properties are specific to the Babylon.js framework during the export and will not interfere with the Blender renders (something interesting to tell to your 3D artists):

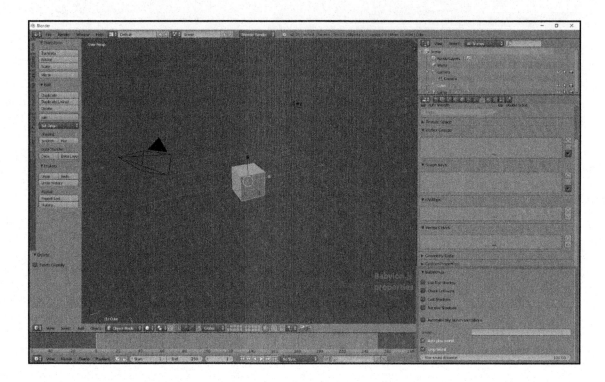

Zoom on the properties:

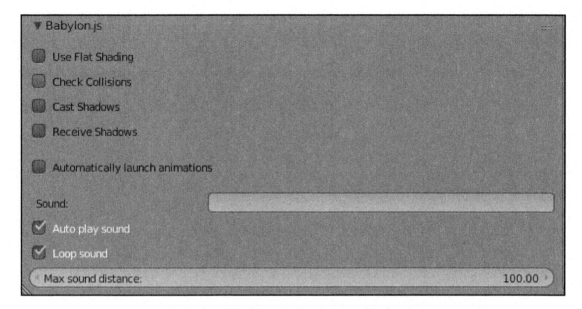

For meshes (such as the cube), the properties are as follows:

- **Use Flat Shading**: This is to use flat shading instead of smoothening the mesh
- **Check Collisions**: This is to check whether the camera collides with the mesh or not
- **Cast Shadows**: This is to check whether the object projects its shadow on other meshes if a shadow light (another type of light) is present in the scene
- **Receive Shadows**: This is to check whether the object receives shadows from other objects that cast shadows if a shadow light is present in the scene
- **Automatically launch animations**: If the mesh is animated, it automatically launches the mesh's animations at the start

Now, select the camera in Blender and let's have a look at the following screenshot:

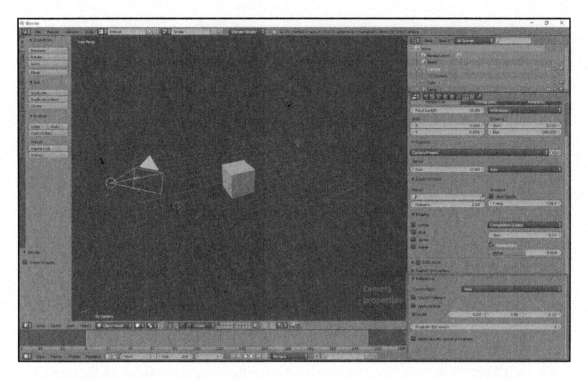

Zoom on the properties:

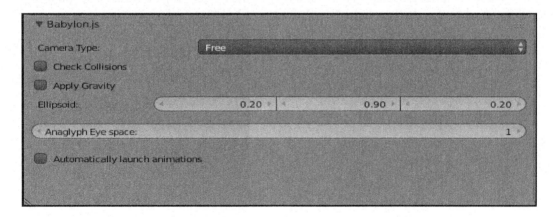

For cameras, the properties are as follows:

- **Camera Type**: This is the type of camera such as free camera (FPS), arc rotation camera, and others
- **Check Collisions**: This is to check whether the camera should check collisions on objects that enable the Check Collisions property
- **Apply Gravity**: This is applied if the gravity should attract the camera
- **Ellipsoid**: This is the radius around the camera where you can check the collisions on the axes (*X*, *Y*, and *Z*)
- **Anaglyph Eye Space**: This is the eye space for anaglyph cameras (anaglyph cameras can be chosen in the Camera Type property)
- **Automatically launch animations**: If the camera is animated, it automatically launches the camera's animations at the start

Select the light in Blender and let's have a look at the following screenshot:

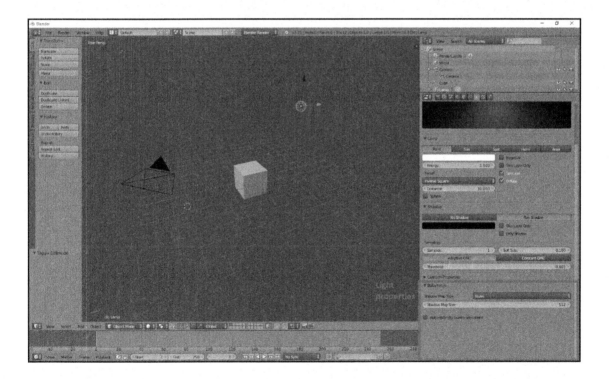

Zoom on the properties:

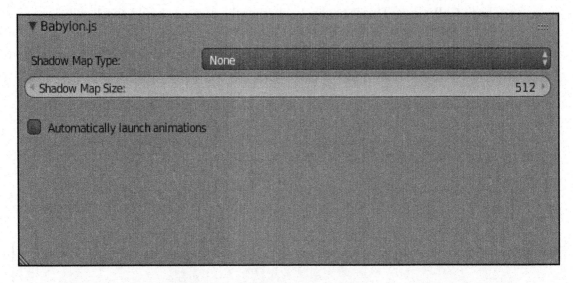

For the lights, the properties are as follows:

- **Shadow Map Type**: If the selection isn't None, the light becomes a shadow light. The variance shadow maps are more expansive than standard shadow maps but they are more realistic.
- **Shadow Map Size**: This is equivalent to the shadow's quality and must be a power of two. 1024 is a good quality for shadows.
- **Automatically launch animations**: If the light is animated, it automatically launches the light's animations at the start.

Let's add a plane to create a ground and export the scene:

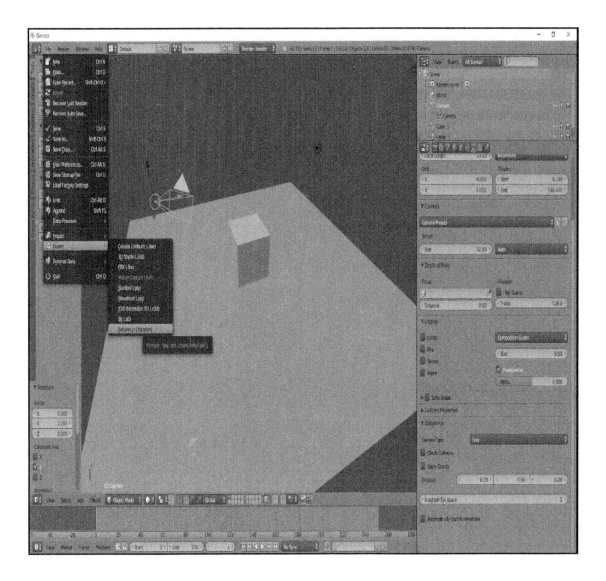

Once you start the exporter, Blender shows you an interface with options on the left-hand side and a file browser (to save the scene file). The options are as follows:

- **Export only current layer**: Blender can handle multiple layers. Check this to export the current layer only.
- **No vertex shading**: This is to disable or enable vertex shading. There will be more information about this in the coming chapters about special effects.

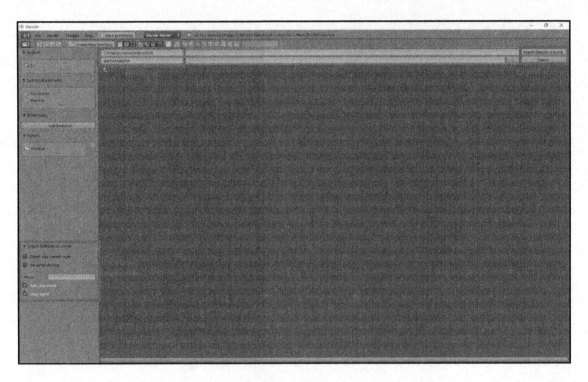

To export the scene, just click on the **Export Babylon.js** scene button.

Once you export the scene, don't hesitate to use the Sandbox tool (http://www.babylonjs.com/sandbox/) to test your scene. Just take the .babylon file and drag and drop the files in the browser. Here is the result:

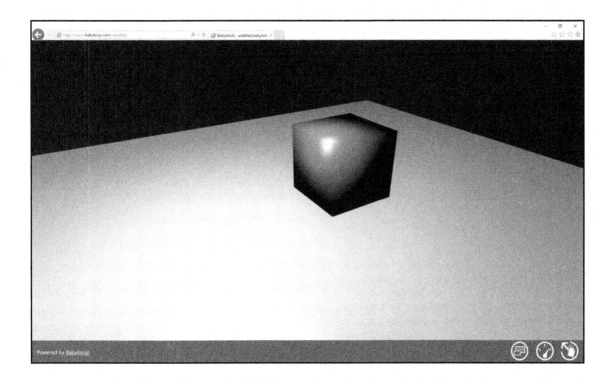

Using 3ds Max to export scenes

As for Blender, you'll find the 3ds Max plugin (written in C#) in the Babylon.js GitHub repository at `Exporters/3Ds Max/Max2Babylon*.zip`, where `*` is the exporter's version. In the archive, you'll find two folders: `2013` and `2015`, that are the currently supported versions of 3ds Max for the `Max2Babylon` exporter.

3ds Max is another tool used by 3D artists to create 3D scenes, such as Blender. 3ds Max is the most famous 3D modeler as it is used for many professional 3D video games and known by all 3D artists.

Installing the Babylon.js exporter for 3ds Max

Once you identify the proper version to use (2013 or 2015), just copy/paste the binaries in the `bin/assemblies` folder and start 3ds Max (typically located at `C:\Program Files\Autodesk\3ds Max 201*\bin\assemblies\`):

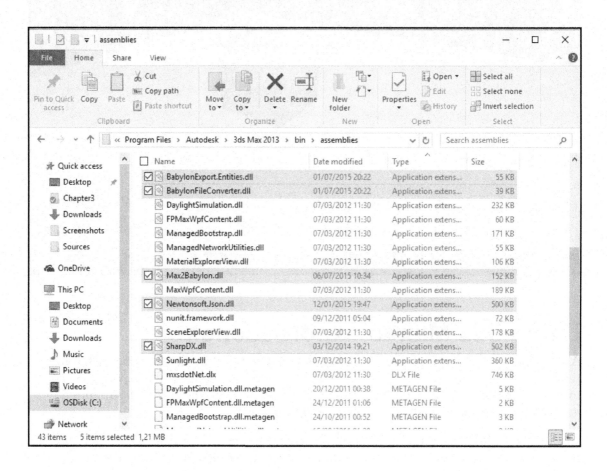

Once you start 3ds Max, a new menu named **Babylon** will appear in the top menu. This menu is used to export the scene to a `.babylon` file. As for Blender, you can modify the Babylon.js properties by right-clicking on the objects in 3ds Max:

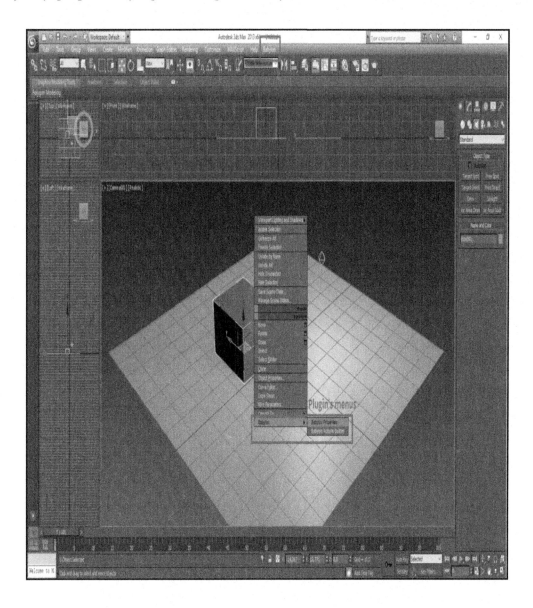

- Zoom on the toolbar:

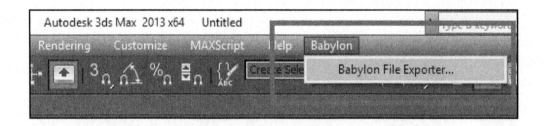

- Zoom on the context menu:

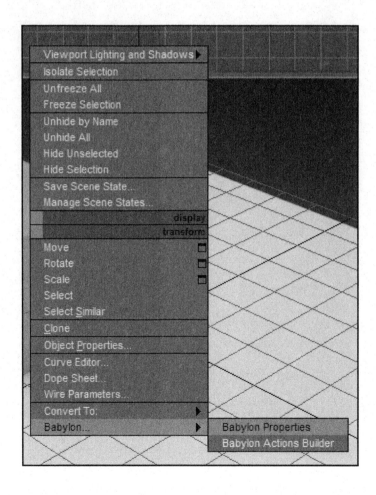

Modifying the properties

The Max2Babylon plugin adds two more menus due to the right-clicking: **Babylon Properties** and **Babylon Actions Builder**.

Actions Builder is a tool that helps create actions on the objects. Let's wait for Chapter 7, *Defining Actions on Objects* to know more about how to create actions on the objects in the scene. For example, Actions Builder was used was used to create actions on objects in the Mansion scene, available at http://babylonjs.com/demos/mansion/.

The properties can be modified on meshes, lights, cameras, and scenes (no object selected). You'll retrieve the same properties as you did for Blender. Just click on the **Babylon Properties** menu.

 Note: some properties including Physics and Sound will be presented in Chapter 5, *Create Collisions on Objects* and Chapter 6, *Manage Audio in Babylon.js* respectively.

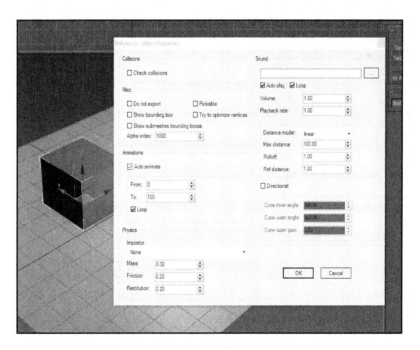

For meshes, there are new properties as follows:

- **Do not export**: This is used if the mesh should get exported to the scene file.

- **Show bounding box**: This is for the purpose of debugging and shows a wireframe box that represents the hull of the mesh.
- **Show submeshes bounding boxes**: As for the **Show bounding box** option, this option will show the bounding boxes of the sub-meshes of the selected mes.
- **Pickable**: This is used if Babylon.js should be able to pick the mesh. Babylon.js allows you to launch rays in the scene and finds the intersection of the ray with the meshes in the scene. Check this to allow picking. For example, mesh picking can be used to select a mesh in a scene when the user clicks on it.
- **Auto animate**: This is used if the object (light, mesh, or camera) is animated at the start.
- **From** and **to**: This is the start frame and end frame of the animation at the start.
- **Loop**: This is used if the animation should be looped.

Select the light in 3ds Max and let's have a look at the following screenshot:

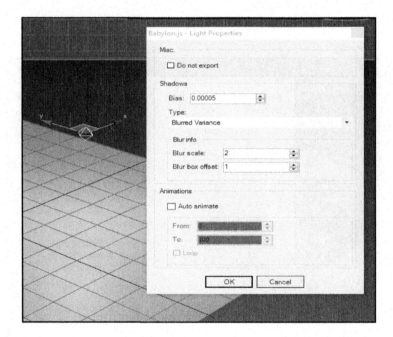

For lights, the properties are equivalent to Blender:

- **Do not export**: This is used if the light should be exported to the scene file.
- **Bias**: This is used to remove the possible artifacts created by the shadow's effect. The default value should be sufficient in most cases.

- **Type**: as for Blender, tells if the light should compute shadows in the scene or not. The `variance` and `blurred variance` shadow maps are more expansive than standard shadow maps but they are more realistic.
- **Blur info**: This is used if the shadow map type is **Blurred Variance**. **Variance shadow maps (VSM)** are more realistic than hard shadows and can be blurred to suppress artefacts.

Select the camera in 3ds Max and let's have a look at the following screenshot:

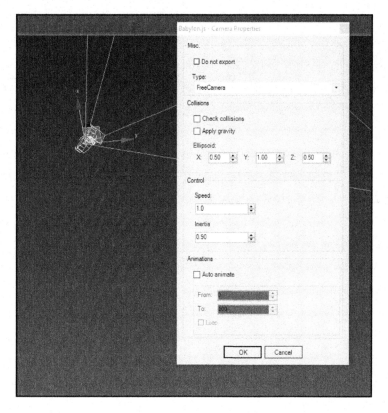

For cameras, the added properties are as follows:

- **Speed**: This is the camera's speed.
- **Inertia**: All cameras in Babylon.js move with an inertia, which represents the inertia of the camera. This means that when you move the camera in Babylon.js, you give it a movement speed that will be slowed according to its inertia value. (means slowed directly, no inertia, and more than means that the camera will

need more time to slow down.)

Exporting the scenes

Let's create the same scene as we did for Blender: a plane, cube, camera, and light:

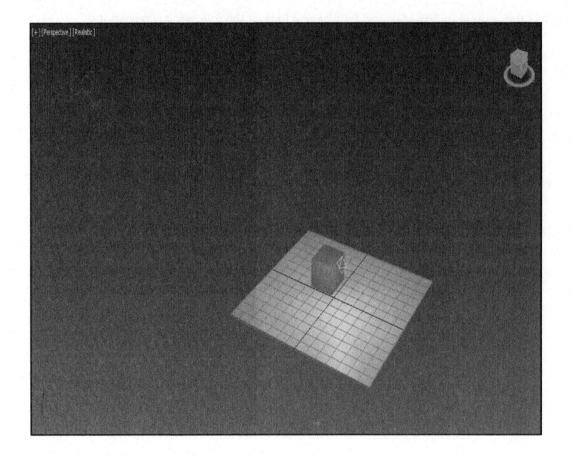

To export this scene, just open the exporter's window using the top menu, **Babylon**:

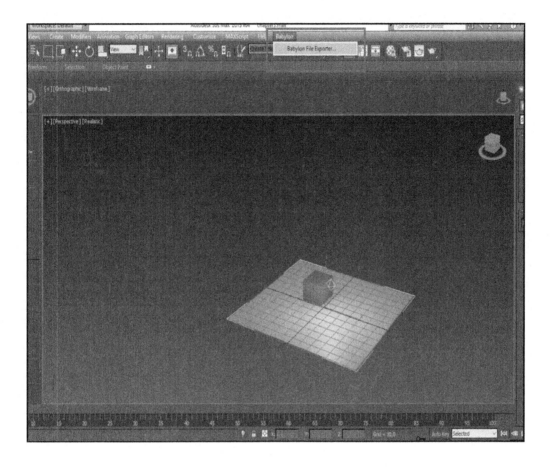

Zoom on the top menu:

The exporter window will appear and let's have a look at the following screenshot:

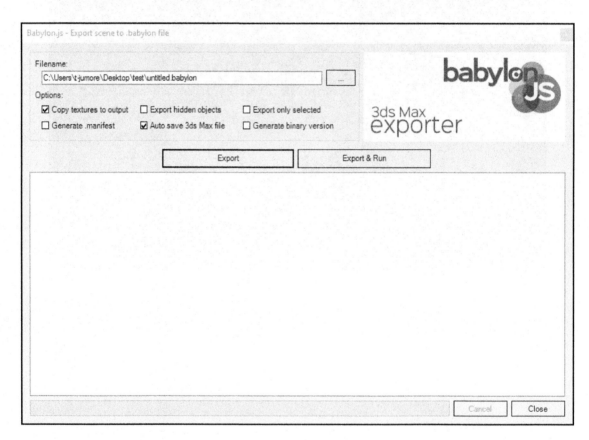

The options are as follows:

- **Copy textures to output**: Check this to export the textures (if any mesh has at least one texture) to the output directory of the scene file. In other words, all the textures of the 3ds Max scene (applied to meshes) will be copied into the same folder as the exported Babylon.js scene file.

- **Generate .manifest**: The manifest files are used for the offline mode with Babylon.js. The exported scenes can be loaded through the Internet and web browser cache as well to save the connection. The manifest files tell the client whether the scene has changed or not. If changed, it just reloads the entire scene through the Internet.

- **Export hidden objects**: In 3ds Max, objects can be hidden (not drawn). This option configures the exporter to keep or export the hidden objects.

- **Auto save 3ds Max file**: At each export, this saves the 3ds Max project.

- **Export only selected**: This exports the selected objects only (meshes, cameras, lights, and so on) to the scene file.

- **Generate binary version**: This exports the scene to a binary file (incremental loading).

Select the file location as you did for Blender to save the Babylon.js scene and click on **Export**. The 3ds Max plugin also offers to export and run the scene by launching the default browser with a local server. The result is as follows:

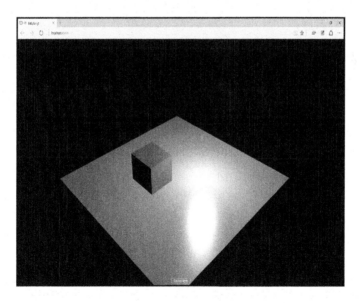

Loading scenes with Babylon.js programmatically

To load scenes using TypeScript, Babylon.js provides you with a class named `BABYLON.SceneLoader`. This class contains static methods that allow you to load scenes (create new ones), append scenes, and load meshes.

Basically, as a developer, you'll load files using these methods. The `.Load` method creates a new scene for you and loads everything (meshes, lights, particle systems, camera, and so on), returning the new scene. The `.Append` method takes an existing scene as a parameter and appends a new scene to the existing one (useful to mix multiple scenes). Finally, the `.ImportMesh` method imports only meshes, skeletons (refer to Chapter 9, *Create and Play Animations* about animations), and particle systems to an existing scene. The following steps will show you how to use these methods and find the right way to manage your scenes.

The BABYLON.SceneLoader class

Loading a scene: The way to load scenes is pretty easy. Just call the `BABYLON.SceneLoader.Load` method with its arguments and let Babylon.js do the rest.

The following is an example:

```
BABYLON.SceneLoader.Load("./", "awesome_scene.babylon", engine);
```

The first argument, `./`, is the scene file folder. The second argument, `awesome_scene.babylon`, is the name of the scene file to load. Finally, the last argument is the engine. Indeed, the loader needs an engine to create a new scene.

Appending a scene: The way to append a scene to another scene is almost the same; just call the `BABYLON.SceneLoader.Append` method instead of `.Load`.

The following is an example:

```
BABYLON.SceneLoader.Load("./", "another_awesome_scene.babylon", scene);
```

The two first arguments are equivalent to the `.Load` method. The last scene parameter is the original scene. Indeed, the new scene created by the loader will be merged with the original one (append).

Importing meshes: Here, the method is different but still located in the `SceneLoader` class with the .ImportMesh method. A scene file (.babylon) contains multiple meshes in the range [0,*n*]. By default, the .Load and .Append methods import all the meshes defined in the scene file. With .ImportMesh, you can specify which meshes are imported by the loader by giving their names.

The following is an example:

```
BABYLON.SceneLoader.ImportMesh("", "./", "awesome_meshes.babylon", scene);
```

The first argument, named meshesNames, is in the any type. Here, the empty string tells the loader to import all the meshes. To specify the meshes to be imported, just add their names in an array, for example, ["awesome_mesh1", "awesome_mesh2"]. The second and third arguments are equivalent to the .Load and .Append methods. The last parameter is the scene to import the meshes to.

The callbacks

The three methods, .Load, .Append, and .ImportMesh, provide callbacks on success, progress, and error that are null by default. They are used to take control of the loading process.

For .Load and .Append, the callbacks are the same.

Load and append

Let's look at the following example:

```
// Same for append
BABYLON.SceneLoader.Load("./", "awesome_scene.babylon", engine,
(scene: BABYLON.Scene) => {
  // Success, with "scene" as the new scene created by the loader
  // We can load another scenes here
}, () => {
  // progress
}, (scene: BABYLON.Scene) => {
  // error, with "scene" as the new scene created by the loader
}
```

The success and error callbacks provide the new scene created by the loader. Indeed, if you take a look at the Babylon.js sources, you can see that the .Load method is just a call to the .Append method by creating a new scene.

Importing a mesh

Let's look at the following example:

```
BABYLON.SceneLoader.ImportMesh("", "./", "awesome_meshes.babylon", scene,
(meshes, particleSystems, skeletons) => {
  // Success, the callback provide access to the new imported meshes,
  // particle systems and skeletons.
}, () => {
  // Progress
}, (scene: BABYLON.Scene, e: any) => {
  // Error callback, access the error with "e"
});
```

In the success callback, the meshes, `particleSystems`, and `skeletons` arguments are arrays of `BABYLON.Mesh`, `BABYLON.ParticleSystem`, and `BABYLON.Skeletons`, respectively and contain only the added objects:

- The meshes argument contains all the imported meshes from the scene file.
- The `particleSystems` argument contains all the imported particle systems (smoke, rain, and others).
- The skeletons argument contains all the imported skeletons. Skeletons are entities used to create animations and are linked to meshes. Let's take a character as an example: the skeleton represents the character's armature and is used to create movements of the legs, hands, head, and so on. Finally, a character can walk and run using the skeletons.

Summary

Now, all tools have been installed and are ready to use. Do not hesitate to take a look at the example files to experiment with the scene loader. There are some example (scene) files including a skull and the scene building with 3ds Max. Naturally, you'll find how to use the scene loader in your code and then get the proper architecture.

As the next step, it is a good occasion to introduce the notion of materials and how to customize the 3D object's appearance using these materials. Of course, Babylon.js already provides you with a default material that makes the work on materials easier than creating materials yourself.

4
Using Materials to Customize 3D Objects Appearance

The objects that we call *materials* are essential in 3D rendering. They are used to render objects on the screen and how they are rendered. This means that the materials are used to apply textures and transformations such as waves, for example, manage transparency and more. In other words, materials are interfaces that are used to easily customize the 3D object's appearance.

The following is an example with Babylon.js:

```
myMesh.material = new BABYLON.StandardMaterial("material", scene);
// Done! Now customize everything you want here
myMesh.material.diffuseTexture = diffuseTexture;
myMesh.material.transparency = 0.5;
// Etc.
```

We will be covering the following topics in this chapter:

- Discussing the awesome theory behind the materials
- Using the Babylon.js standard material
- Using textures with materials

Discussing the awesome theory behind the materials

The materials are used to customize 3D objects appearance; however, behind them lie two programs called **shaders**. The goal of materials is to hide this notion of shaders and simply work with the values in the material object. In other words, the values in the material can be the emissive color of the object, the diffuse color, the transparency level and so on.

In fact, to go further with the theory, there are several types of shader, as shown in the following list:

- **Vertex Shader**: This works directly on the 3D object geometry.
- **Pixel Shader**: This works directly on the pixels on the screen.
- **Geometry Shader** (not available on WebGL): This works on the 3D object geometry; however, here it is able to directly add polygons to the geometry of the 3D object according to the output of the vertex shader.
- **Compute Shader** (not available on WebGL): This doesn't work directly on the 3D objects and pixels. It is just used to compute some user-defined data using the GPU instead of the CPU. For example, a compute shader will take a texture as the input (you can see that as a big matrix) and output the results of the program in another texture. The compute shader is highly used, for example, to compute realistic ocean waves or neural networks.
- **Tesselation Shader** (not available on WebGL): This allows us to compute **Level of Detail** (**LOD**) directly on the GPU instead of the CPU (fairly new in the modern rendering pipelines, such as Direct3D 11 and OpenGL 4.0).

In our case and with WebGL, only the vertex and pixel shaders are used to render 3D scenes on the screen; however, it would not be surprising to see the other types of shaders being implemented in WebGL in the future.

The theory

The meshes that we created in the previous chapters contain vertex buffers and index buffers. The vertex buffers describe the 3D positions of the vertices. The main problem is how to project the vertices in a 3D space into a 2D space, which is the screen space. Indeed, to draw elements on the screen, GPUs are used through programs to transform the vertices positions into 2D positions on the screen. These programs are the vertex shader and the pixel shader. They are written with a language named GLSL, which is the OpenGL shading language used with WebGL.

The vertex shader

The vertex shader is used to transform the vertices positions. It is executed by the GPU for each vertex and can be used for an infinite number of functions. For example, to create waves on a large ocean plane, we will use the vertex shader to compute the wave function for each vertex instead of using the TS code that is executed on the CPU side–leave the job to the real worker.

Once the vertex shader computes a triangle (a face) on the screen, thanks to the index buffer, the pixel shader is called to illuminate the pixels used by the current triangle (current face) of the current mesh that is rendered.

The pixel shader

The pixel shader has the same structure as the vertex shader; it is written with the same language (GLSL) and is called for each pixel used by the current triangle on the screen. The main function of the pixel shader is to return a color computed in the RGBA format, which can be determined from a user-defined value or directly from a texture.

Using the Babylon.js standard material

Babylon.js allows you to create materials, which means that it can create the custom materials with custom shaders; however, it provides a standard material with already-developed shaders that are designed to be adapted by many customizations.

In fact, when you add a light to a Babylon.js scene, the light properties such as diffuse color, are sent to the materials of the scene to compute the light contributions on the meshes.

The standard material and its common properties

In Babylon.js, each mesh has a material and the meshes can share the same material. Creating a standard material and assigning it to a mesh with Babylon.js is as easy as writing the following:

```
myMesh.material = new BABYLON.StandardMaterial("materialName", scene);
```

Simply create a new `StandardMaterial` object by giving a name to the material and the scene where you want to add the material and assign it `the.material` property of a mesh. Once the material is created, you can start modifying the values and then customize the mesh appearance. The default material by default looks similar to the following image:

- The diffuse color: The diffuse color represents the color of the object, as follows:

```
myMaterial.diffuseColor = new BABYLON.Color3(0, 0, 1); // Blue
```

- The specular color: The specular color represents the light color reflected by the object (this is mixed with the diffuse color), as shown in the following:

```
myMaterial.specularColor = new BABYLON.Color3(1, 0, 0); // Red
```

- The emissive color: The emissive color represents the color emitted by the object (this is mixed with the specular color and the diffuse color), as follows:

```
myMaterial.emissiveColor = new BABYLON.Color3(0, 1, 0); // Green
```

- Manage transparency: To manage transparency, the standard material provides a .alpha property in the [0, 1] interval, as follows:

```
myMaterial.alpha = 0.2; // 80% transparent
```

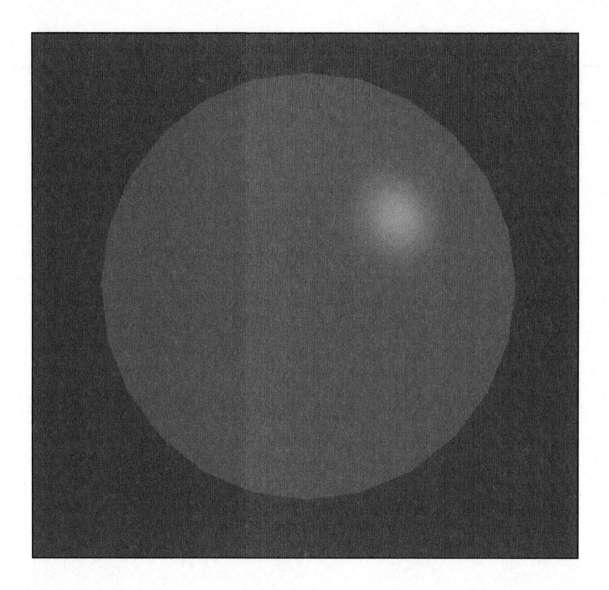

Using the fog

The standard material allows you to apply the fog effect that is related to the current scene that is rendered. To enable the fog on an object, simply set the.fogEnabled property to true on the materials and the scene, as shown in the following:

```
myMaterial.fogEnabled = true;
```

```
scene.fogEnabled = true;
```

Let's start with the following scene:

The fog in a scene can be customized. There are several types of fog, as shown in the following:

- Linear fog (BABYLON.Scene.FOGMODE_LINEAR)
- Exponential (BABYLON.Scene.FOGMODE_EXP)
- Exponential 2 (faster than the previous) (BABYLON.Scene.FOGMODE_EXP2)

With the linear mode, the two properties—scene.fogStart and scene.fogEnd—can be set. Consider the following, as an example:

```
scene.fogMode = BABYLON.Scene.FOGMODE_LINEAR;
scene.fogStart = 10;
scene.fogEnd = 100;
```

Change the fog color using the following:

```
scene.fogColor = new BABYLON.Color3(1, 1, 1); // White
```

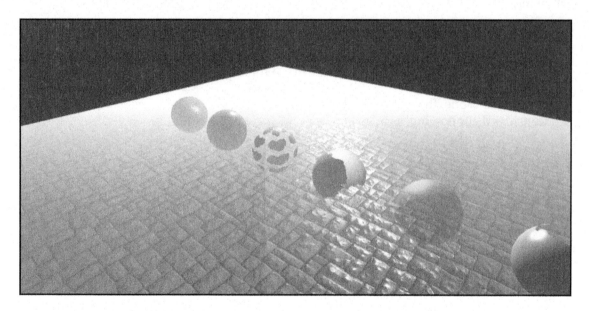

With the exponential mode, the `scene.fogDensity` property can be set.

Consider the following as an example:

```
scene.fogMode = BABYLON.Scene.FOGMODE_EXP;
scene.fogDensity = 0.02;
```

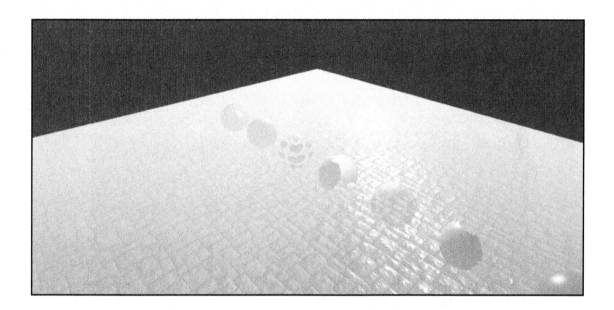

Using textures with materials

This chapter is the right place to introduce the usage of textures. Textures are images (.png,.jpeg, and so on) that graphics libraries are able to apply to meshes. There are several types of texturing methods handled by Babylon.js, such as video textures, cube textures, and so on. Now, let's explain how to use textures with materials.

Load and apply a texture

As you may have already guessed, loading and applying a texture to a mesh can be easy with Babylon.js. The standard material provides a way, as for colors, to apply a diffuse texture (for example, specular, emissive, and ambient textures). Simply set the .diffuseTexture property to the reference of your texture, as follows:

```
myMaterial.diffuseTexture = myTexture;
```

To create the myTexture object, let's take a look at the BABYLON.Texture class, as shown in the following:

```
var myTexture = new BABYLON.Texture("path_to_texture.png", scene);
```

This is done now. The diffuse texture will now be applied to the mesh. Consider the `floor_diffuse.png` image in the example files as an example:

Now, let's play with the texture's properties. In the example files, there is a `cloud.png` texture that contains an alpha channel (transparency). If you apply the cloud texture, the result is as shown in the following image:

The black part represents the alpha channel and looks like an artifact that pollutes the rendering part of the sphere. In fact, the textures are applied on meshes thanks to the pixel shaders, and you must tell the shaders that the textures can contain an alpha channel. This job can be done thanks to the .hasAlpha property of the texture, as follows:

```
cloudTexture.hasAlpha = true;
```

The result is the following image:

You can see that the back faces of the sphere are not rendered. This is due to the optimization of the graphics libraries as it is not necessarily needed (in most cases) to render the triangles of the back faces that the cameras cannot see. It is called `back-face culling`.

To disable the `back-face culling`, simply set the `.backFaceCulling` property of the material to false, as follows:

```
myMaterial.backFaceCulling = false;
```

The result is as shown in the following image:

Since textures are applied by the pixel shaders, a lot of parameters can be set thanks to the materials, for example, the vertical and horizontal scales of the texture. Let's start with the following texture:

The `.uScale` and `.vScale` properties of a texture allow us to apply a repeat pattern to the mesh. The 1.0 default value means that the texture is repeated once on the mesh. Let's see the following result with `5.0`:

```
myTexture.uScale = 5.0;
myTexture.vScale = 5.0;
```

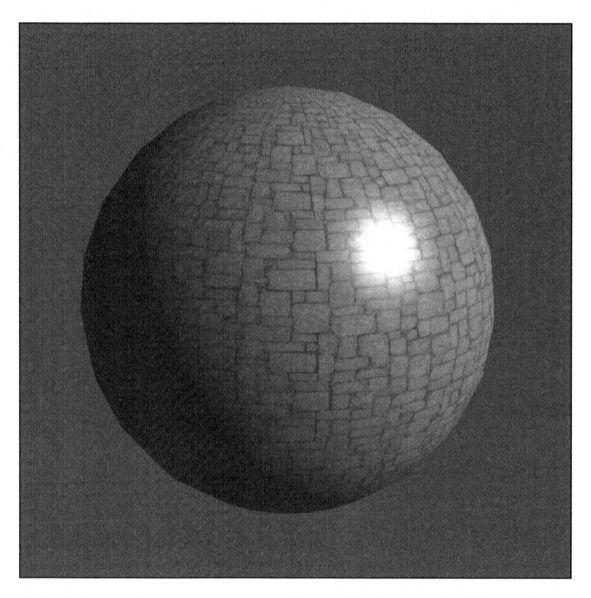

As for the textures scales, you can create an offset to adjust the texture's positions on the mesh according to the `.uScale` and `.vScale` properties, as follows:

```
myTexture.vScale = 0.2;
myTexture.uScale = 0.2;
```

The bump mapping

In the texturing methods that Babylon.js is handling, we can the find the bump mapping technique. This technique is used to create a relief on a surface and have more realistic surfaces using two different textures: the diffuse texture and a *normal texture*. This technique is famous as it doesn't modify the original geometry of the mesh and is only computed by the shaders using the two textures.

The diffuse and normal textures are provided by the artists and are built by some artist's tools to help the production. An example of normal texture is as follows:

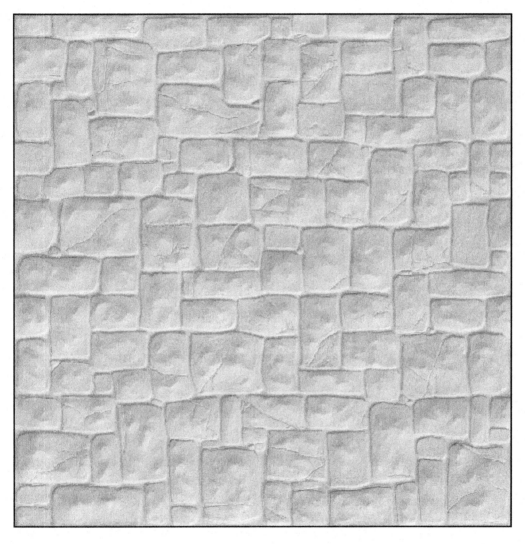

In fact, the pixel shader applies the diffuse texture and modifies the pixels in the function of the normal texture.

Let's see the normal mapping effect. This is without normal mapping:

With normal mapping, the image will look similar to the following:

Applying the normal mapping effect with Babylon.js is as easy as applying a diffuse texture. Let's explain this with the following two lines of code:

```
myMaterial.diffuseTexture = new BABYLON.Texture("diffuse.png", scene);
myMaterial.bumpTexture = new BABYLON.Texture("normal.png", scene);
```

The internal effect of the material is able to adapt the rendering in the function of the properties. Then, if the `.bumpTexture` property is set, the effect will compute the bump mapping technique.

Advanced texturing

The standard material of Babylon.js allows us to apply a reflection texture. If this texture is set, the internal effect of the material will create a reflection effect using this texture.

The cube texture

The cube texture is special. An interesting use of the reflection texture with a cube texture is the skybox mesh. A skybox is composed of six faces and tends to reproduce the environment around a scene, typically the sky. To handle the six faces with a texture, the cube texture will load six textures and apply them to the mesh.

Let's load a cube texture with Babylon.js, as follows:

```
var cubeTexture = new BABYLON.CubeTexture("skybox/TropicalSunnyDay",
scene);
```

The parameters are as shown in the following:

- The path to the six textures. Each texture name must begin with `TropicalSunnyDay` in this example, followed by the six directions of the cube: `nx`, `ny`, `nz`, `px`, `py`, and `pz`.
- The scene where to add the cube texture.

 Note: the default extension for the cube texture is .jpg. You can learn of the precise extension by passing a third parameter, which is an array of String. Consider the following as an example:

```
var cubeTexture = new BABYLON.CubeTexture("skybox/TropicalSunnyDay", scene,
["_px.png", "_py.png", "_pz.png", "_nx.png", "_ny.png", "_nz.png"]);
```

Now, let's create a skybox. A skybox is a cube with `back-face culling` disabled as the camera will be in the cube, as follows:

```
var skybox = BABYLON.Mesh.CreateBox("skybox", 300, scene);
```

```
var skyboxMaterial = new BABYLON.StandardMaterial("skyboxMaterial", scene);
skyboxMaterial.backFaceCulling = false;
skyboxMaterial.reflectionTexture =
  new BABYLON.CubeTexture("skybox/TropicalSunnyDay", scene);
```

In the result, the cube texture is applied to the cube; however, we can find some artifacts in the links between parts of the cube texture:

These artefacts are due to the coordinates mode of the texture. In fact, the textures are applied to meshes by the 2D coordinates provided by the mesh's geometry. As for the vertex buffer and the index buffer, the geometry contains a coordinate buffer commonly named the **UVs** buffer, and several methods exist to apply a certain coordinate pattern. In this case, the skybox coordinate mode should be applied. This is possible with the `.coordinatesMode` property, as follows

```
myTexture.coordinatesMode = BABYLON.Texture.SKYBOX_MODE;
```

Once the coordinates mode is set, the result looks great, as shown in the following image:

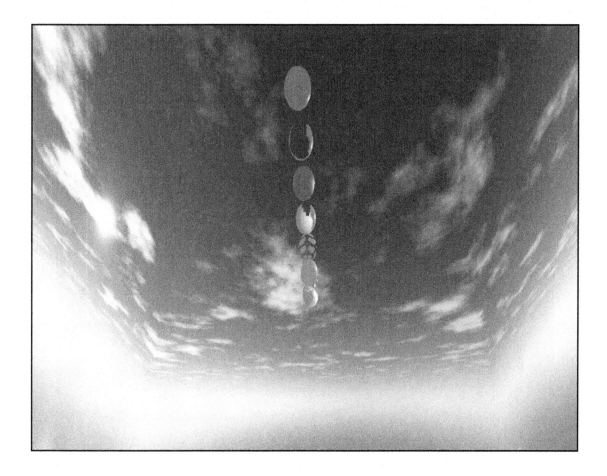

The result of the skybox outside the cube is as follows:

The mirror texture

Let's explain the usage of a reflection texture with a new texture type named **Mirror Texture**. With Babylon.js, it is possible to reflect the world using a mirror texture. The mirror texture is particular as it is created by Babylon.js and can render the scene into a texture. Behind the reflection texture, a new texture type is used: the render target texture. Render target textures are used to directly render meshes into a texture for further use.

Now, let's create a mirror texture, as follows:

```
var mirror = new BABYLON.MirrorTexture("mirror", 512, scene);
```

The parameters are as shown in the following:

- The texture name: The name of the texture created by Babylon.js.
- The texture size: The bigger the texture, the cleaner the mirror texture is. Unfortunately, bigger the texture, bigger will be its impact on the performance. The values 512 or 1024 (512 x 512 or 1024 x 1024 pixels) are good sizes for a mirror texture.
- The scene where to add the texture.

Now, to reflect the world, the mirror texture needs a last parameter: the mirror plane. If we take the ground as an example, we want the ground to reflect the world above itself:

```
mirror.mirrorPlane = BABYLON.Plane.FromPositionAndNormal(
    new BABYLON.Vector3(0, 0, 0), new BABYLON.Vector3(0, -1, 0));
```

A plane has four properties: a, b, c, and d. The first three properties represent the normal vector, where d is the distance to the origin. The FromPositionAndNormal static method is a helper to create a plane. The parameters are as follows:

- The plane's position vector. Here, the origin (x=0, y=0, z=0).
- In the example files, the plane position is (x=0, y=-5, z=0). Therefore, the plane's position must be (x=0, y=5, z=0).
- The plane's normal vector. Here, the origin is (x=0, y=-1, z=0).

Then, the code lines become the following:

```
var mirror = new BABYLON.MirrorTexture("mirror", 512, scene);
mirror.mirrorPlane = BABYLON.Plane.FromPositionAndNormal(
    new BABYLON.Vector3(0, 0, 0),
new BABYLON.Vector3(0, -1, 0));
myMaterial.reflectionTexture = mirror;
```

To configure the render target texture in the mirror texture, we must provide an array of BABYLON.AbstractMesh. This array is used to render only the meshes indexed in the array. The array is already created by the mirror texture and the property's name is .renderList. Then, the mirror texture will only expose the added meshes in the array, as follows:

```
mirror.renderList.push(myMesh1);
mirror.renderList.push(myMesh2);
// Etc.
```

The result with a ground (plane at the same position) and the reflected spheres is as shown in the following image:

Summary

In this chapter, you saw what materials are, the theory about what is happening backstage, and how to use the standard materials of Babylon.js. You saw that using a material in Babylon.js is also easy.

The example files tend to reproduce the notions viewed in this chapter: colors, alpha, textures, fog, back-face culling, and so on. Now, you can practice with materials and customize appearance of meshes.

As a concrete example, the materials are highly used in all the 3D scenes and configured by 3D artists: if we take a scene of Babylon.js made by Michel Rousseau, where he used two meshes and two different materials to reproduce the following image:

The first mesh is the body of the vase with a standard material applied to it and the second mesh represents the embers with another standard material applied to them. Each material is configured with a different diffuse texture. If we set the body as `isVisible = false`, we can see how the embers look in reality, as shown in the following image:

Finally, all the meshes rendered in this scene are using standard materials, configured with different values and textures, to finally look similar to the following image:

In the next chapter, you'll create your first scene with an FPS camera and collisions management. You will learn how to manage collisions between objects and how to manage physics with Babylon.js.

5

Create Collisions on Objects

The previous chapters introduced the 3D programming basics and Babylon.js. You can easily create and customize your scenes using the materials and meshes provided by your designer as you now understand the complete workflow.

In this chapter, let's play with the gameplay itself and create interactions with objects in the scene by creating collisions and physics simulations. Collisions are important to add realism to your scenes if you want to walk without crossing the walls. Moreover, to make the scenes more alive, let's introduce the physics simulation with Babylon.js and finally, see how easy it is to integrate these two notions in your scenes:

- Checking collisions in a scene
- Simulatating physics

Checking collisions in a scene

Starting from the concept, configuring and checking collisions in a scene can be done without mathematical notations. We all have the notion of gravity and ellipsoid, even if the *ellipsoid* word is not necessarily familiar.

How collisions work in Babylon.js?

Let's start with the following scene (a camera, light, plane, and box):

The goal is to prevent the currently active camera of the scene from crossing the objects in the scene. In other words, we want the camera to stay above the plane and stop moving forward if it collides with the box.

To perform these actions, the collisions system provided by Babylon.js uses a **collider**. A collider can be represented by the `bounding box` of a simple object and it looks similar to the following image:

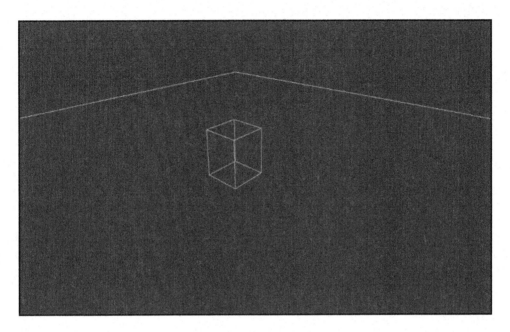

For information, a bounding box simply represents the minimum and maximum positions of a mesh's vertices and it is computed automatically by Babylon.js.

As explained in `Chapter 3`, *Create, Load, and Draw 3D Objects on the Screen*, the meshes are composed of vertices that are linked together using the index buffer to finally build triangles; to be precise, the collisions are based on these triangles and are automatically managed/computed by Babylon.js. This means that you have to do nothing that is particularly tricky to configure collisions with objects.

To resume, all the collisions are based on the triangles of each mesh in order to determine whether the camera should be blocked or not.

 You'll also see that the physics engines use the same kind of collider to simulate physics for simple meshes (bounding boxes).

In this case, the complicated part is for the designer. They must optimize all their meshes to work well with the collisions. This means that they must split the big meshes into multiple or submeshes thanks to their 3D modeler.

In fact, when rendering the scene, the collision system of Babylon.js will test whether the collisions should be tested for each mesh in the scene according to the global position of the camera. This is how 3D engines tend to optimize collisions as the main problem is that the collisions are computed in the CPU side.

For example, some 3D engines offer a way to configure collisions on meshes by giving a particular type of collision; even if the mesh is complex, you can choose whether you want to use a bounding box as collider (to save the CPU performances) or directly use the triangles of the mesh (realistic collisions).

Configuring collisions in a scene

Let's practice with the Babylon.js collisions engine itself. You'll see that the engine is particularly well-hidden as you only have to enable checks on the scene and objects.

Firstly, configure the scene in order to enable the collisions and then wake the engine up. If the following property is `false`, all the next properties will be ignored by Babylon.js and the collisions engine will be in the *stand by* mode. Then, it's easy to enable or disable the collisions in a scene without modifying more properties, as follows:

```
scene.collisionsEnabled = true; // Enable collisions in scene
```

Next, configure the camera to check the collisions. The collisions engine will check collisions for all the rendered cameras that have collisions enabled. Here, we have only one camera to configure:

```
camera.checkCollisions = true; // Check collisions for THIS camera
```

To finish, set the `.checkCollisions` property of each mesh to `true` to activate collisions (here, the plane and box), as shown in the following:

```
plane.checkCollisions = true;
box.checkCollisions = true;
```

Now, the collisions engine will check the collisions in the scene for the camera on both plane and box meshes.

You guessed right , if you want to enable collisions only on the plane and want the camera to move across the box, you'll have to set the `.checkCollisions` property of the box to `false`, as follows:

```
plane.checkCollisions = true;
box.checkCollisions = false;
```

Configure gravity and ellipsoid

Gravity

In the previous section, the camera checks the collision on the plane and the box; however, this is not submitted to a famous force named **the gravity**. To enrich the collisions in your scene, you can apply the gravity force, for example, to go down from the stairs.

First, enable the gravity on the camera by setting the `.applyGravity` property to `true`, as shown in the following:

```
camera.applyGravity = true; // Enable gravity on the camera
```

Finally, customize the gravity direction by setting `BABYLON.Vector3` to the `.gravity` property of your scene, as follows:

```
scene.gravity = new BABYLON.Vector3(0.0, -9.81, 0.0); // To stay on earth
```

Of course, the gravity in space should be as shown in the following:

```
scene.gravity = BABYLON.Vector3.Zero(); // No gravity in space
```

Don't hesitate to play with the values in order to adjust the gravity to your scene referential.

Ellipsoid

The last parameter to enrich the collisions in your scene is the camera's ellipsoid. The ellipsoid represents the camera's dimensions in the scene. In other words, it adjusts the collisions according to the x, y, and z axes of the ellipsoid (an ellipsoid is represented by `BABYLON.Vector3`).

For example, the camera must measure 1.8 m (y axis) and the minimum distance to collide with the x (sides) and z (forward) axes must be 1 m. Then, the ellipsoid must be (x = 1, y = 1.8, and z = 1). Simply, set the `.ellipsoid` property of the camera, as follows:

```
camera.ellipsoid = new BABYLON.Vector3(1, 1.8, 1);
```

> The default value of the camera's ellipsoids is (x = 0.5, y = 1.0, and z = 0.5)

As for the gravity, don't hesitate to adjust the x, y, and z according to your scene scale.

Simulate physics

Physics simulation is pretty different from the collisions system since it does not occur on the cameras but on the objects of the scene itself. In other words, if physics is enabled (and configured) on a box, the box will interact with other meshes in the scene and try to represent the real physical movements.

For example, let's take a sphere in the air. If you apply physics to the sphere, the sphere will fall until it collides with another mesh and according to the given parameters, it will bounce and roll in the scene.

 The example files reproduce the behavior of a sphere that falls on the box in the middle of the scene.

Enable physics in Babylon.js

In Babylon.js, physics simulations can be only done using plugins. Two plugins are available for use: the Cannon.js framework and the Oimo.js framework. These two frameworks are included in the Babylon.js GitHub repository in the `dist` folder.

Each scene has its own physics simulations system and can be enabled by the following lines:

```
var gravity = new BABYLON.Vector3(0, -9.81, 0);
scene.enablePhysics(gravity, new BABYLON.OimoJSPlugin());
// or
scene.enablePhysics(gravity, new BABYLON.CannonJSPlugin());
```

The `.enablePhysics(gravity, plugin)` function takes the following two arguments:

- The gravity force of the scene to apply on objects
- The plugin to use:
  - Oimo.js: `new BABYLON.OimoJSPlugin()`
  - Cannon.js: `new BABYLON.CannonJSPlugin()`

To disable physics in a scene, simply call the `.disablePhysicsEngine()` function, as follows:

```
scene.disablePhysicsEngine();
```

Impostors

Once the physics simulations are enabled in a scene, you can configure the physics properties (or physics states) of the scene meshes. To configure the physics properties of a mesh, the `BABYLON.Mesh` class provides a `setPhysicsState(impostor, options)` function.

The parameters are as follows:

- `impostor`: Each kind of mesh has its own impostor according to its form. For example, a box will tend to slip while a sphere will roll. There are several types of impostors.
- `options`: These options define the values used in physics equations. It counts the mass, friction, and restitution.

Let's consider a box named `box` with a mass of 1 and set its physics properties, as shown in the following snippet:

```
box.setPhysicsState(BABYLON.PhysicsEngine.BoxImpostor, { mass: 1 });
```

That's all, the box is now configured to interact with other configured meshes by following the physics equations. Let's imagine that the box is in the air and will fall until it collides with another configured mesh.

Now, let's take a sphere named `sphere` with a mass of 2 and set its physics properties, as shown in the following snippet:

```
sphere.setPhysicsState(BABYLON.PhysicsEngine.SphereImpostor, { mass: 2 });
```

You'll notice that the sphere, which is a particular kind of mesh, has its own impostor (`SphereImpostor`). In contrast to the box, the physics equations of the plugin will make the sphere roll, while the box will slip on other meshes.

According to their masses, if the box and sphere collide, then the sphere will tend to push the box harder .

The following impostors are available in Babylon.js:

- The box impostor: `BABYLON.PhysicsEngine.BoxImpostor`
- The sphere impostor: `BABYLON.PhysicsEngine.SphereImpostor`
- The plane impostor: `BABYLON.PhysicsEngine.PlaneImpostor`
- The cylinder impostor: `BABYLON.PhysicsEngine.CylinderImpostor`

In fact, in Babylon.js, the box, plane, and cylinder impostors are the same according to the Cannon.js and Oimo.js plugins. It exists other kinds of physics bodies that are not yet supported (but maybe soon) in the physics engine of Babylon.js; for example, the soft bodies (such as a flag which is deformed due to the wind) and the liquid bodies (simulating the behavior of an object on a water surface according to its mass and the water's properties, such as clear or watery). Only rigid bodies are supported here at the moment.

Regardless of the `impostor` parameter, the `options` parameter is the same. You can customize the physics state of a mesh by providing the following parameters:

- **The mass**: This is the mass of the mesh in the world. The heavier the mesh is, the harder it is to stop its movement.
- **The friction**: This represents the force opposed to the meshes in contact. In other words, this represents how the mesh is slippery. To give you an order, The value of the friction for the ice is equal to `1.0`. We can determine that the friction is in the `[0, 1]` range.
- **The restitution**: This represents how the mesh will bounce on others. Consider a ping-pong ball and its table; if the table's material is a carpet, the restitution will be small. However, if the table's material is a glass, the restitution will be maximum. A real interval for the restitution is in `[0, 1]`.

In the example files, these parameters are set and if you play with them, you'll see that these three parameters are linked together in the physics equations.

Applying a force to a mesh

At any moment, you can apply a new force or impulse to a configured mesh. Let's take an explosion for example, a box is located at the ($x = 0, y = 0$, and $z = 0$) coordinates and an explosion takes place above the box at the ($x = 0, y = -5$, and $z = 0$) coordinates. In real life, the box would be pushed up; this action is possible by calling a `applyImpulse(force, contactPoint)` function provided by the `BABYLON.Mesh` class.

Once the mesh is configured with its options and impostor, you can call this function at any moment to apply a force to the object. The parameters for this are as follows:

- `force`: This represents the force in the x, y, and z axes
- `contact point`: This represents the origin of the force located in the x, y, and z axes.

For example, the explosion generates a force only on y (why not?), which is equal to 10 (10 is an arbitrary value) and has its origin at the ($x = 0, y = -5,$ and $z = 0$) coordinates, as follows:

```
mesh.applyImpulse(new BABYLON.Vector3(0, 10, 0), new BABYLON.Vector3(0, -5, 0));
```

Once the impulse is applied to the mesh (only once), the box is pushed up and it will fall according to its physics parameters (mass, friction, and restitution).

Configuring in Blender and 3ds Max

Going back to the 3D software such as Blender and 3ds Max that are used by the artists, it's also possible to configure collisions and physics simulations.

Collisions in Blender

Starting from this scene, the collisions are easy to configure, as shown in the following screenshot:

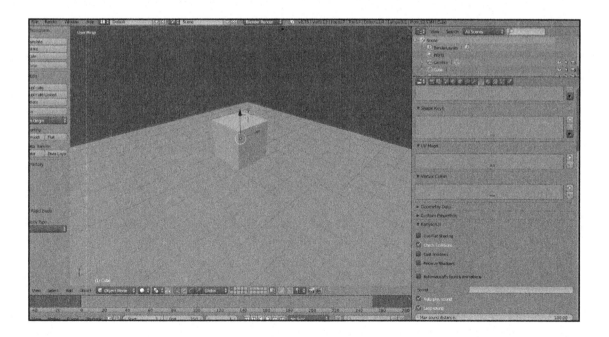

For Chapter 3, *Create, Load, and Draw 3D Objects on the Screen*, let's zoom on the Babylon.js properties, as shown in the following image:

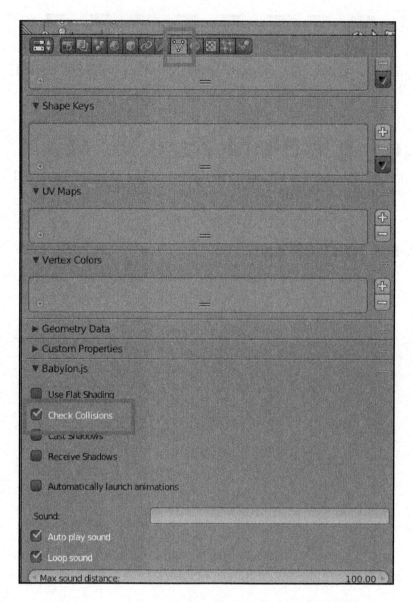

First, click on the options button (at the top) and for the selected object, which is the cube here, enable the collisions by checking the **Check Collisions** check box. For every mesh, check the checkbox to enable the collisions.

Now, let's configure the camera in Blender. Select the camera in the scene, click on the camera's options (at the top), and check the **Enable Collisions** and **Apply Gravity** check boxes if you want to apply gravity on your camera, as shown in the following image:

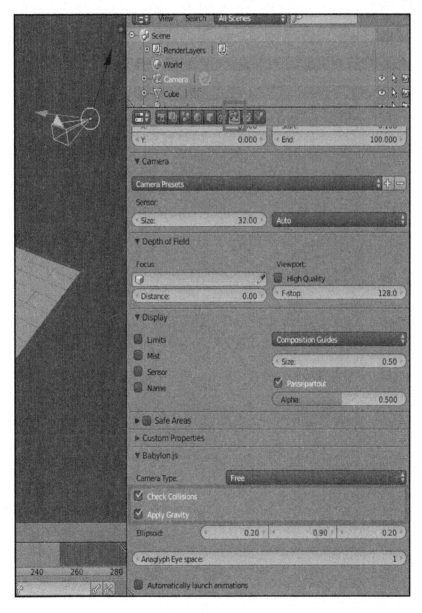

To configure the camera's ellipsoid, a `BABYLON.Vector3` dialog is available under the two check boxes. You can configure the x, y, and z values of the camera's ellipsoid in the same order.

Finally, if you want to apply gravity to your camera, the last parameter to configure is the scene's gravity. First, click on the scene menu (at the top) and modify the gravity values. In Blender, the y and z axes are switched, therefore, the z-axis of the gravity in Blender corresponds to the y-axis in Babylon.js, as shown in the following image:

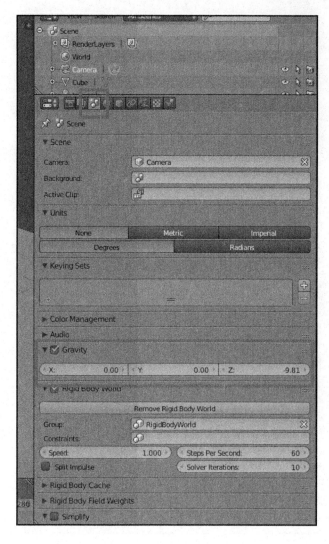

You can now export the Blender project and test it; the gravity will be applied and the camera will check the collisions on the cube and plane.

Configuring physics simulations in Blender

As for the collisions system, you can configure the meshes in Blender in order to simulate physics. You'll find the notions of impostor, mass, friction, and restitution, and all these parameters can be configured in Blender. Once you select a mesh, click on the physics options (at the top) and click on the **Rigid Body** button (only rigid bodies are supported), as shown in the following image:

Once you click on the button, more options will appear. Some of these options are relative to Blender; however, only some of them will interest us, as shown in the following:

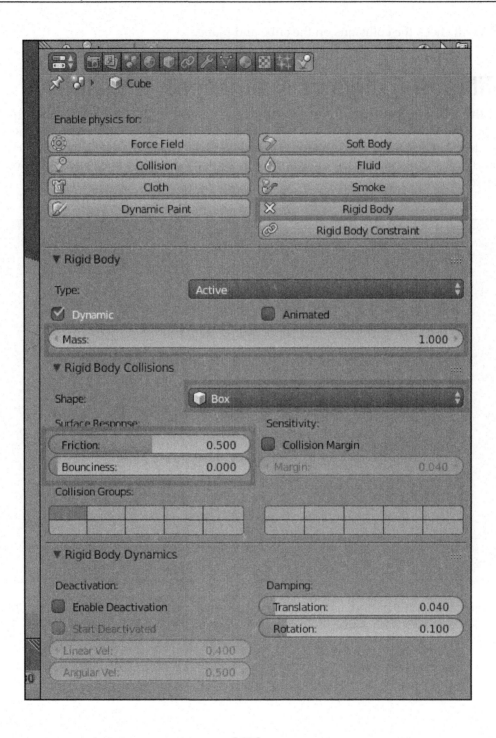

You'll find the three parameters (options): the mass, friction, and bounciness (bounciness represents the restitution). In Blender, the impostor is called shape and you'll find the same impostors: Box and Sphere.

Configuring collisions in 3ds Max

As for Blender, you can configure collisions in 3ds Max. To enable collisions on an object, simply open the Babylon properties of the mesh, as shown in the following image:

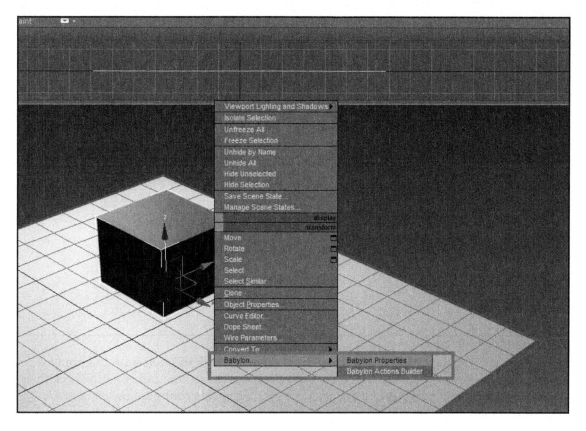

To enable collisions on the mesh, simply check the **Check collisions** check box, as shown in the following image:

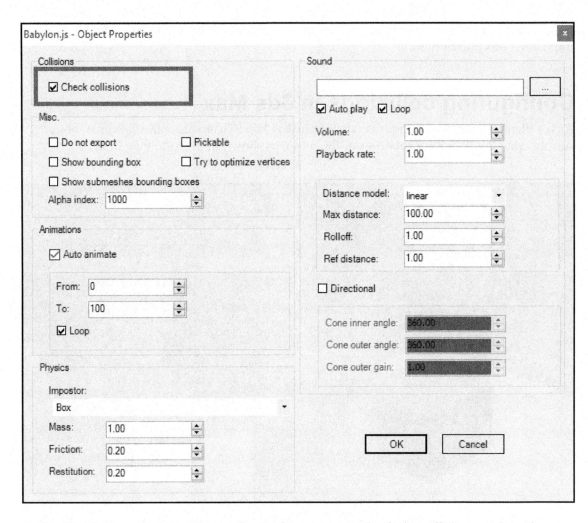

As for Blender, you have to also configure the camera to check the collisions and apply gravity (or not). As for the mesh, open the Babylon properties of the camera and check the **Check collisions** and **Apply gravity** check boxes. You can also configure the camera's ellipsoid on the x, y, and z axes in the same order, as shown in the following image:

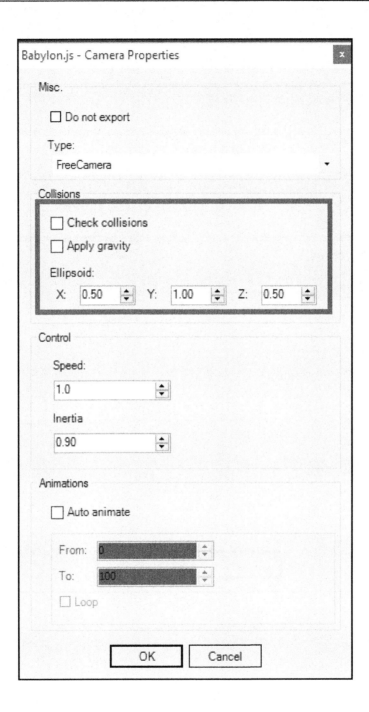

Finally, open the Babylon properties of the 3ds Max scene to configure the gravity if you want to apply gravity to the camera, as follows:

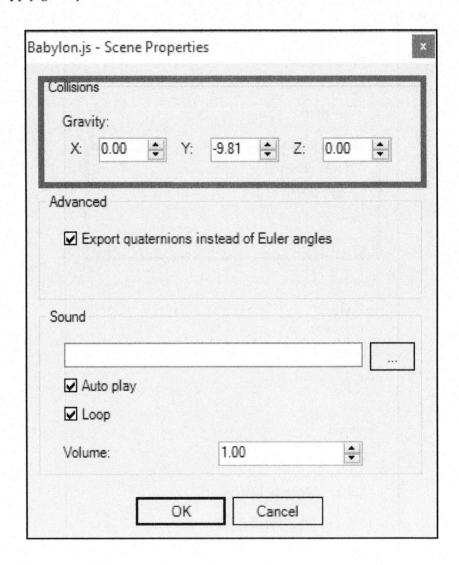

Configuring physics simulations in 3ds Max

In 3ds Max, the physics properties are located in the Babylon mesh properties in contrast to Blender. Simply select a mesh and open the Babylon properties. You'll find the same notions of impostor, mass, friction, and restitution, as shown in the following screenshot:

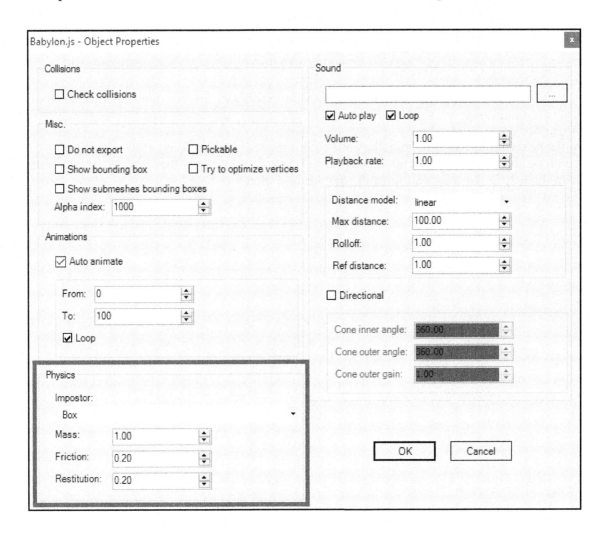

Summary

You are now ready to configure the collisions for your scene and simulate physics. Whether by code or by artists, you can understand the pipeline in order to make your scenes more alive. Don't hesitate to manipulate the example files. There are three important functions, as follows:

- `createScene()`: This creates the meshes and materials
- `createCollisions()`: This configures the collisions on scene, camera, and meshes
- `createPhysics()`: This configures the physics properties of meshes and applies impulses

In the next chapter, it's time to make your scenes more alive by adding audio tracks to it. You'll be able to add sounds, spatialized or not, to your scenes whether by code or by artists with the help of the sound support in 3ds Max and Blender.

6
Manage Audio in Babylon.js

In the last chapter, you started adding dynamism to your scenes by adding collisions checks and physics simulations. Another important feature is handling sounds in your scenes and finally making it more alive. This chapter not only explains sound management with Babylon.js in order to create soundtrack sounds, but also spatialized sounds (3D). In this chapter, we will cover the following topics:

- Playing 2D sounds
- Playing 3D sounds

Playing 2D sounds

The Babylon.js framework provides an audio engine based on WebAudio. It allows you to easily add 2D and 3D sounds using the provided tools that are developed for you by the Babylon.js team.

Creating 2D sounds

The Babylon.js framework provides a `BABYLON.Sound` class. This class allows you to create and manage 2D and 3D sounds for your scene. To add a sound, the only thing you need to do is to create a new `BABYLON.Sound` object, as follows:

```
var sound = new BABYLON.Sound("sound_name", "sound_file", scene);
```

You can now get access to methods such as `.play`, `.pause`, and `.stop`.

In fact, the sounds are loaded asynchronously so that you cannot call `sound.play()` right after creating the new sound object. This is why the `BABYLON.Sound` constructor provides a readyToPlayCallback parameter after the scene in order to handle the loading process. To play the sound when loaded, simply set the readyToPlayCallback parameter, as follows:

```
var sound = new BABYLON.Sound("sound_name", "sound_file", scene, () => {
    sound.play();
});
```

Fortunately, the developers thought about this behavior and provided a last parameter named options. This parameter allows you to automatically set the default behaviors instead of managing them in the ready-to-play callback. The options parameter is optional and is an object that looks similar to the following:

```
var sound = new BABYLON.Sound("sound_name", "sound_file", scene, () => {
}, {
    loop: true, // [Boolean] plays sounds in loop mode
    autoPlay: true, // [Boolean] plays the sound after loading
    volume: 1.0, // Between [Number [0, 1]] volume of sound
    playbackRate: 1.0 // [Number 1.0] playing speed
    spatialSound: false, [Boolean] is a 3D sound
    maxDistance: 100, [Boolean] maximum distance of 3D sound
});
```

The autoPlay parameter will automatically play the sound when loaded and you don't have to manage the sound in the ready-to-play callback.

The Babylon.js framework still keeps things simple as you already added an audio track to your scene only by calling a new statement on the BABYLON.Sound class.

Of course, you can play several sounds in a single scene, as shown in the following code:

```
var options = {
    loop: true,
    autoPlay: true
};
var sound1 = new BABYLON.Sound("sound1", "sound1.mp3", scene, null,
options);
var sound2 = new BABYLON.Sound("sound2", "sound2.mp3", scene, null,
options);
```

Managing 2D sounds

There are several properties to manipulate a sound in 2D , such as the volume, whether the sound is playing or not, and so on.

To set the sound's volume, just call the `.setVolume` function of the sound. The new volume is set in the [0, 1] interval, as shown in the following code:

```
sound.setVolume(0.5);
```

You can also get the volume, as shown in the following code:

```
var currentVolume = sound.getVolume();
```

You can check the current state of a sound any time, as follows:

```
sound.isPlaying; // true if the sound is playing
sound.isPaused // true if the sound was paused
```

You can also set the sound's state any time, as follows:

```
sound.play(); // Plays the sound
sound.pause(); // Pauses the sound
sound.stop(); // Stops the sound
```

Playing 3D sounds

In the previous topic, you added and played 2D sounds in a scene. These 2D sounds can be easily used as soundtracks for your games. To add dynamism to your scenes, as physics and collisions do, you can configure the sounds to be spatialized in a scene. The spatialized sounds, which are called 3D sounds, give give the notion of distance and orientation between the player and the sound. In other words, more the player is far from the sound, more the sound will be attenuated. Also, if the sound position is rather on the right of the player, the right speaker will generate more sound than the left speaker and vice versa.

For example, if the sound is emitted on your right, only the right speaker(s) should play it and the farther you are from the sound, the lower the sound's volume should be.

Creating 3D sounds

You can imagine that, as for the 2D sounds, you can create a spatialized sound using the same `BABYLON.Sound` constructor. Only the `options` parameter will change as you have to set `spatialSound` to `true`, as follows:

```
var sound = new BABYLON.Sound("sound", "sound_file", scene, () => {
    sound.play();
}, { spatialSound: true });
```

Once you have created the spatialized sound, you can set its 3D position in the scene's world using a BABYLON.Vector3, as follows:

```
sound.setPosition(new BABYLON.Vector3(0, 0, 50)); // For example
```

Managing 3D sounds

In contrast to the 2D sounds, you can customize more properties with 3D sounds. Spatialized sounds provide properties to configure the attenuation and panning model.

For example, the default distance model (attenuation) is set to be linear. Two other models such as exponential and inverse exist, as follows:

```
sound.distanceModel = "exponential";
```

As for the fog (Chapter 4, *Using Materials to Customize 3D Objects Appearance*), the linear model says that the farther away the player is from the sound source, the lower the sound will be following a linear function (the threshold of 0 volume is set by the maxDistance property). The exponential model is a variant of the linear model by following an exponential function.

The maxDistance property can be set only if the distance model is linear, as follows:

```
sound.updateOptions({
maxDistance: 10 // If the player's distance to the sound is >= 10 then the
volume will be 0
});
```

As for the maxDistance property, you can set the rolloffFactor property if you're using an exponential model, as shown in the following code:

```
sound.updateOptions({
rolloffFactor: 2
});
```

Of course, you can update multiple values at the same time. Just configure the .updateOptions parameter with the values. Consider the following as an example:

```
sound.updateOptions({
maxDistance: 10,
rolloffFactor: 2
});
```

The last useful function for spatialized sounds is to directly attach a sound to a mesh. Then, it is not required to update the sound's position manually to set it to the mesh's position, as follows:

```
sound.attachToMesh(myMesh);
```

Now, the sound and mesh share the same position and are updated together by the scene when you call `scene.render()`.

Creating a directional spatialized sound

The previous spatialized sounds that you created were omnidirectional. This means that if you are behind a speaker, you'll hear the sound as loud as when you are in front of the speaker. Something that does not happen in real life. The Babylon.js audio engine provides a way to create directional sounds that are easily configurable.

Note that direction-spatialized sounds work only when the sound is attached to a mesh.

Let's start with the following sound reference:

```
var sound = new BABYLON.Sound("sound", "sound_file", scene, () => {
}, { loop: true, autoplay: true });
```

You can configure it to be directional by calling only three functions.

First, the direction of the sound is represented by a cone. Just set the direction cone, as follows:

```
sound.setDirectionalCone(90, 180, 0.1); // Values are in degree
```

There are three parameters, which are as follows:

- The size of the inner cone (in degrees) should be smaller than the outer cone
- The size of the outer cone (in degrees) should be larger than the inner cone
- The volume of the spatialized sound when the player is outside the outer cone

For a perfect directional sound, the sizes of the inner and outer cone should be equal.

Once the directional cone is set, just set the direction of the sound according to the mesh rotation. The parameter is local to the mesh. Then, if you rotate the speaker, for example, the sound will always follow the speaker's rotation, depending on the parameter. Consider the following example:

```
sound.setLocalDirectionToMesh(new BABYLON.Vector3(0, 0, 1)); // Always
speak ahead (Z is the forward axis)
```

Finally, don't forget to attach the sound to the mesh, as follows:

```
sound.attachToMesh(myMesh); // myMesh should be the speaker in the example
```

Summary

This quick chapter demonstrates that using sounds (2D and 3D) in a 3D engine can be easy when powerful tools are provided to the developer. The example files create a 2D sound that is played as a soundtrack and a 3D sound located at the box's position. Do not hesitate to play with the distance models and check the effects using your headphones.

In the next chapter, we'll try to automate some things using the `ActionManager` class of Babylon.js. This class is useful for executing actions on objects when a trigger is raised. For example, if the player left-clicks on the box, it plays the sound named `my_sound.wav`. It's also the time to introduce **Actions Builder**, which is a part of the Babylon.js 3ds Max exporter. Actions Builder allows artists (and developers) to create actions on their objects without any lines of code.

7
Defining Actions on Objects

Let's go further with the gameplay in Babylon.js. The framework provides an `ActionManager` class that allows us to manage and execute actions when a trigger is raised by the engine.

For example, imagine a scene with a button. When the button is pushed (left-click), the light(s) in the scene should be turned off, except one. This is only an example. In this chapter, we will cover the following topics:

- Defining actions on objects
- Using conditions to control the actions graph
- Using the Actions Builder in 3ds Max

Defining actions on objects

The Babylon.js framework comes with a collection of distinct actions. You'll find actions that can play a sound, stop a sound, interpolate a property of an object, set a value of an object property, and so on.

Enable actions on an object

The only entities that can handle `ActionManager` are the scene and the meshes in the scene. Each Babylon.js mesh has its own action manager reference. To enable actions on a mesh, just create a new reference to the mesh, as follows:

```
myMesh.actionManager = new BABYLON.ActionManager(scene);
```

The `ActionManager` constructor takes only the scene as a parameter.

Let's create your first action in a scene composed of a box and a plane. The action must change the box's position on the *y* axis from to 6 when the user left-clicks on the box. The only thing to do is to call the `.registerAction` function on `ActionManager` of the box, as shown in the following:

```
myMesh.actionManager = new BABYLON.ActionManager(scene);
myMesh.actionManager.registerAction(new BABYLON.SetValueAction(
    // The trigger type
    BABYLON.ActionManager.OnLeftPickTrigger,
    // The target
    myMesh,
    // Property to modify
    "position.y",
    // The new value
    6,
    // The condition
    null
));
```

For a moment, let's consider the condition as `null` and explain it in the next topic.

If we look more closely, an action is triggered by a trigger (here, `BABYLON.ActionManager.OnLeftPickTrigger`). There are several types of triggers available only for the meshes, as follows:

- `OnPickTrigger`: When the object is picked (click).
- `OnLeftPickTrigger`: When the object is picked (left-click only).
- `OnRightPickTrigger`: When the object is picked (right-click only).
- `OnCenterPickTrigger`: When the object is picked (mouse wheel click only).
- `OnPointerOverTrigger`: When the pointer is over the object (entering).
- `OnPointerOutTrigger`: When the pointer is out of the object (exiting).
- `OnIntersectionEnterTrigger`: When the object intersects another object.
- `OnIntersectionExitTrigger`: When the object finishes intersecting another object.
- `NothingTrigger`: Only used for chained actions. Let's see the next sub-topic.

 Note: all picking triggers require that meshes are pickable: `myMesh.isPickable = true;`

Also, there are several types of triggers available only on scenes. Indeed, scenes can have `ActionManager` as well, as follows:

- **OnEveryFrameTrigger**: This raises the associated actions in every frame rendered by Babylon.js
- **OnKeyDownTrigger**: When the user presses a key (keyboard)
- **OnKeyUpTrigger**: When the user finishes pressing a key (keyboard)

As you can guess, some triggers need parameters. Triggers such as `OnIntersectionEnterTrigger`, `OnIntersectionExitTrigger`, `OnKeyDownTrigger` and `OnKeyUpTrigger`. To configure a trigger that needs parameters, just provide a JavaScript object that will contain the trigger type and the parameter, instead of the giving directly the trigger type as argument in the action's constructor. Consider the previous example with `OnIntersectionEnterTrigger` in the following:

```
myMesh.actionManager.registerAction(new BABYLON.SetValueAction(
  // The trigger, the structure is the same for
  // OnIntersectionExitTrigger
  {
    trigger: BABYLON.ActionManager.OnIntersectionEnterTrigger,
    parameter: myOtherMeshReference
  }, // The target
  myMesh,
  // Property to modify
  "position.y",
  // The new value
  6,
  // The condition
  null
));
```

For the `OnKeyDownTrigger` and `OnKeyUpTrigger`, the structure is the same and the parameter is the key. Consider the following for example:

```
myMesh.actionManager.registerAction(new BABYLON.SetValueAction(
  // The trigger, the structure is the same for
  // OnKeyUpTrigger
  {
    trigger: BABYLON.ActionManager.OnKeyDownTrigger,
    parameter: "d" // When the user pushes the key "d"
  },
  // The target
  myMesh,
  // Property to modify
  "position.y",
  // The new value
  6,
  // The condition
  null
```

```
));
```

Let's look more closely at the following parameters of an action:

- **The trigger**: This determines when the action is triggered by the action manager. You can see the trigger as an event type.
- **The target**: This represents the object (not necessarily a mesh or a scene in all the cases; however, a JavaScript object in general) that will be modified by the action.
- **The property to modify**: This represents the property of the target that will be modified by the action.
- **The new value**: This represents the new value affected to the property of the target. This can be a number, string, object, and so on.

Almost all the available actions work with these parameters.

Chain actions on an object

The `ActionManager` class of Babylon.js allows you to construct a graph of actions. All the registered actions will be checked (to verify the trigger) and executed (if the check concludes) at same time and repeatedly. However, imagine the following as your scenario:

When the user left-clicks on the box, the new position on the *y* axis is and when the user left-clicks once again on the box, the new rotation on the *y* axis is `PI / 4`.

The second action (left-click again) must be executed only when the first action is executed. To perform this action, you can call the `.then` function in an action. Consider the following as an example:

```
myMesh.actionManager.registerAction(new BABYLON.SetValueAction(
    BABYLON.ActionManager.OnLeftPickTrigger,
    myMesh,
    "position.y",
    6,
    null
    )
    // Will be executed on the second left-click
    .then(new BAYBLON.SetValueAction(
    BABYLON.ActionManager.NothingTrigger,
    myMesh,
    "rotation.y",
    Math.PI / 4,
    null
));
```

This method is available for all actions.

The available actions

Now, let's enumerate all the available actions, as follows:

- `BABYLON.SwitchBooleanAction`: This switches a Boolean property (false to true, or true to false). Consider the following, for example:

```
new BABYLON.SwitchBooleanAction(trigger, target,
    propertyToModify (boolean), condition);
```

- `BABYLON.SetValueAction`: This sets a new value to the property, similar to the preceding examples.
- `BABYLON.IncrementValueAction`: This increments the value of a property (only available with number values) by the specified value. Consider the following for example:

```
new BABYLON.IncrementValueAction(trigger, target,
    propertyToModify (number), valueToIncrement)
```

- `BABYLON.PlayAnimationAction`: This plays an animation available in the object, such as a character or button must be `BABYLON.Node`. Chapter 9, *Create and Play Animations* for how to set up and play with animations. Consider the following, for example:

```
new BABYLON.PlayAnimationAction(trigger, target, startFram
    e, endFrame, loop);
```

> Animations work with frames, from 0 to 200, for example. The action specifies the start frame and end frame (25 to 35, for example). The loop parameter is a Boolean that specifies if the played animation is looped.

- `BABYLON.StopAnimationAction`: This stops the animation of the target object. Consider the following example:

```
new BABYLON.StopAnimationAction(trigger, target);
```

- `BABYLON.DoNothingAction`: This does nothing. It is used to control the graph and bypass a click, for example. Consider the following example:

```
new BABYLON.DoNothingAction(trigger);
```

- `BABYLON.ExecuteCodeAction`: This executes your own function. Consider the following example:

```
new BABYLON.ExecuteCodeAction(trigger, (evt: ActionEvent) =>          {
    console.log("executing action !");
    console.log(evt.source);
    console.log(evt.pointerX);
    console.log(evt.pointerY);
    console.log(evt.meshUnderPointer);
    console.log(evt.sourceEvent);
    console.log(evt.additionalData);
});
```

- `BABYLON.SetParentAction`: This sets a new parent for the target object. The target must be BABYLON.Node (mesh, light, camera, and so on). Consider the following example:

```
new BABYLON.SetParentAction(trigger, target,
    theParentReference);
```

- `BABYLON.PlaySoundAction`: This plays a sound. Just provide a `BABYLON.Sound` reference. Consider the following example:

```
new BABYLON.PlaySoundAction(trigger, theSoundReference);
```

- `BABYLON.StopSoundAction`: This stops a sound. Just provide the `BABYLON.Sound` reference. Consider the following example:

```
new BABYLON.StopSoundAction(trigger, theSoundReference);
```

- `BABYLON.InterpolateValueAction`: This interpolates a value (creates an animation) of the target object `BABYLON.Node`. Consider the following example:

```
new BABYLON.InterpolateValueAction(trigger, target,
    propertyToInterpolate, finalValue, durationInMS);
```

> The property to interpolate must be of the `number, BABYLON.Color3, BABYLON.Vector3, or BABYLON.Quaternion` type.

> For example, the property to interpolate can be `position` and the value `new BABYLON.Vector3(0, 6, 0)`.

- `BABYLON.CombineAction`: This is a special action. It allows simultaneous execution of multiple actions anywhere in the graph. Consider the following example:

```
new BABYLON.CombineAction(trigger, childrenActions);
```

childrenActions is an array of BABYLON.Action. It contains the simultaneously executed actions.

Using conditions to control the actions graphs

In the previous sub-topic (the available actions), the conditions in actions were bypassed. In fact, every action can have a condition that controls whether the ActionManager executes the action or not. The conditions can check whether a value is one of the following states compared to another value:

- Equal
- Lesser
- Greater
- Different

There are three types of condition, as follows:

- **State condition**: This checkswhether the .state property of BABYLON.Node is equal to the given state. A state is a string.
- **Value condition**: This checkswhether a property is equal, lesser, greater, or different from a given value.
- **Predicate condition**: This calls a custom method that will return true or false.

If an action has a condition, the action will be executed only if the condition returns true.

Adding conditions to your actions graph shows all the power of the Actions Builder, which comes in the next topic. To understand the following example, before practicing with conditions, you can access this demo (http://www.babylonjs.com/Demos/ActionBuil der/) made by the artist Michel Rousseau, who used only actions and conditions to create the interactions in the scene.

The principle is that you must activate the three buttons in order to turn the main light off.

As a developer, the theory is as follows:

- When the user clicks on a button (OnLeftPickTrigger for each button):
    - If the button is pressed (StateCondition), un-press the button

and turn off the light (`SetValueAction`)
- If the button isn't pressed (`StateCondition`), press the button and turn on the light (`SetValueAction`)
- At every frame (`OnEveryFrameTrigger`):
  - If the three buttons are pressed (chained `StateCondition`), set the main light's diffuse color to black (turn off) (`SetValueAction`)
  - If one of the three buttons isn't pressed (`StateCondition` on each button), set the main light's diffuse color to white (turn on) (`SetValueAction`)

The theory can be performed with actions by chaining the conditions (to check whether the three buttons are pressed) and the actions in the graph. Of course, the Actions Builder will allow you to have a real representation on the graph instead of having it in your mind. You'll just have to manipulate it to train and learn the proper way to think with actions.

State condition

The state conditionchecks whether the `.state` property of `BABYLON.Node` is equal to the given state.

Consider the following example with `BABYLON.StateCondition`:

```
myMesh.state = "isUp";
// If mesh state is "isDown", make position.y up
var condition1 = new BABYLON.StateCondition(myMesh.actionManager,
myMesh, "isDown");
myMesh.actionManager.registerAction(new BABYLON.SetValueAction(
  BABYLON.ActionManager.OnLeftPickTrigger, myMesh,
    "position.y", 6, condition1);
// Else if mesh state is "isUp", make position.y down
var condition2 = new BABYLON.StateCondition(myMesh.actionManager,
  myMesh, "isUp");
myMesh.actionManager.registerAction(new BABYLON.SetValueAction(
  BABYLON.ActionManager.OnLeftPickTrigger, myMesh,
    "position.y", 0, condition2);
```

Predicate condition

The predicate condition executes a custom function that will return true or false. It is particularly useful if the condition has to test multiple values or manipulate objects using TypeScript before it returns true or false. Let's create the same example as we did earlier using a predicate condition, as follows:

```
myMesh.position.y = 6;
// If mesh position.y is 6, set it to 0
var condition1 = new BABYLON.PredicateCondition(myMesh.actionManag
er, () => {
  return myMesh.position.y === 6;
});
myMesh.actionManager.registerAction(new BABYLON.SetValueAction(
  BABYLON.ActionManager.OnLeftPickTrigger, myMesh,
    "position.y", 0, condition1);
// Else if mesh position.y is 0, set it to 6
var condition2 = new BABYLON.PredicateCondition(myMesh.actionManag
er, () => {
  return myMesh.position.y === 0;
});
myMesh.actionManager.registerAction(new BABYLON.SetValueAction(
  BABYLON.ActionManager.OnLeftPickTrigger, myMesh,
    "position.y", 6, condition2);
```

Value condition

The value condition is a way to automatically check whether a value is equal, lesser, greater, or different without writing a predicate condition. Let's create the previous example again using BABYLON.ValueCondition, as follows:

```
myMesh.position.y = 6;
// If mesh position.y is 6, set it to 0
var condition1 = new BABYLON.ValueCondition(myMesh.actionManager,    myMesh,
  "position.y", 6, BABYLON.ValueCondition.IsEqual);
myMesh.actionManager.registerAction(new BABYLON.SetValueAction(
  BABYLON.ActionManager.OnLeftPickTrigger, myMesh, "position.y", 0    ,
condition1);
// Else if mesh position.y is 0, set it to 6
var condition2 = new BABYLON.ValueCondition(myMesh.actionManager, myMesh,
  "position.y", 0, BABYLON.ValueCondition.IsEqual);
myMesh.actionManager.registerAction(new BABYLON.SetValueAction(
  BABYLON.ActionManager.OnLeftPickTrigger, myMesh, "position.y", 6    ,
condition2);
```

The value condition works like an action, you have to specify the target (myMesh), the property (position.y), and the value to test (and 6).

Using the Actions Builder in 3ds Max

Creating actions can save lines of code. The Babylon.js solution also provides a way for 3ds Max artists and you, as a developer to create actions, including conditions, without any lines of code.

The Actions Builderallowed Michel Rousseau to create actions and scenarios in his scenes without any lines of code, as shown in the following:

- The Mansion scene: `http://www.babylonjs.com/?MANSION`
- The Actions Builder scene: `http://www.babylonjs.com/?AB`

To do this, you can simply use the Actions Builder, which is a part of the 3ds Max plugin of Babylon.js. The Actions Builder is located in the `BabylonActionsBuilder` folder available in the 3ds Max plugin in the GitHub repository. You can copy and paste the folder into the 3ds Max plugins directory, which is typically located at `C:\Program Files\Autodesk\3ds Max 2013\bin\assemblies`, as you can see in the following screenshot:

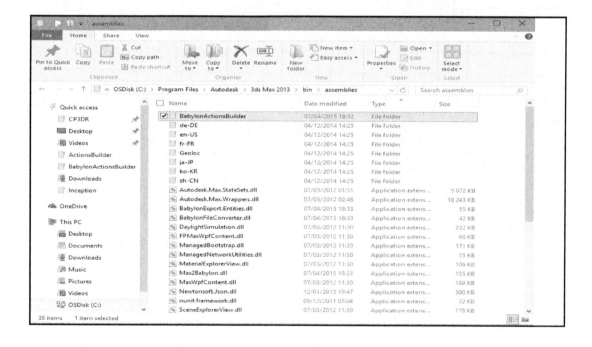

How it works

To use the Actions Builder, simply select an object in 3ds Max, right-click on it, select the **Babylon...** menu, and open **Babylon Actions Builder**.

 Note: To edit the scene actions, select nothing in the 3ds Max scene, right-click on the void, select the **Babylon...** menu, and open **Babylon Actions Builder**.

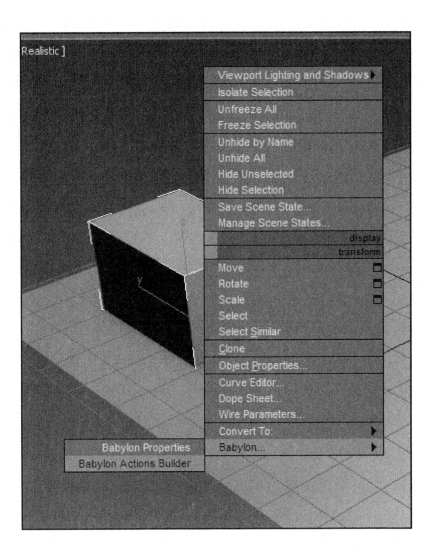

The Actions Builder window appears. You are now able to add actions to your object without any lines of code. In the Actions Builder, all actions are available, except the actions that execute the code
(BABYLON.ExecuteCodeAction and BABYLON.PredicateCondition).

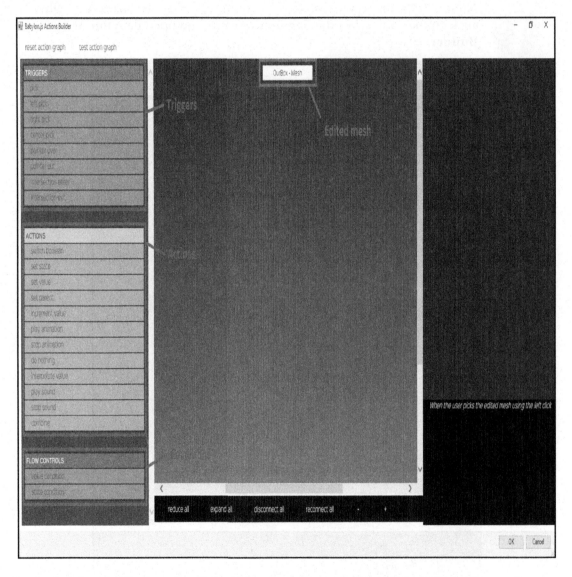

On the left-hand side, there is a list of triggers, actions, and conditions. To add an action or condition, you have to start with a trigger. Simply Drag'n'drop the required trigger on the root node (ourMesh).

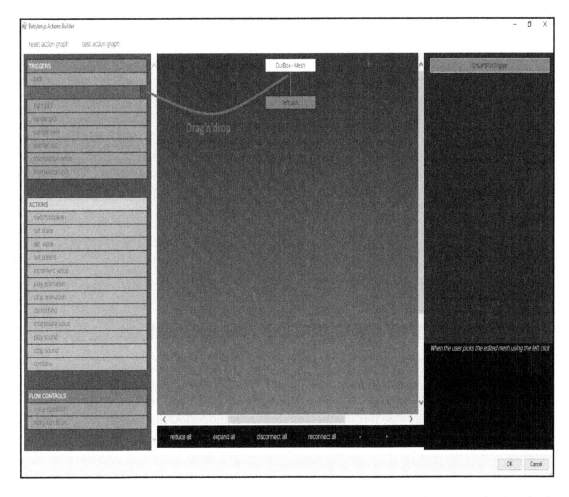

Now, the child action will be executed once the user left-clicks on the **ourBox** object, which is a mesh.

Once you added the wanted trigger, you can *drag'n'drop* any action or a condition in the graph. For example, let's add BABYLON.InterpolateValueAction, as shown in the following image:

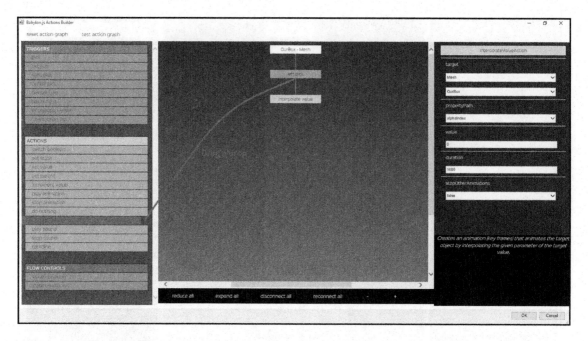

If you click on the added action, a few menus will appear on the right-hand side. These menus will correspond to the parameters of the constructor of the action. You will retrieve the target, property, and value parameters, as shown in the following image:

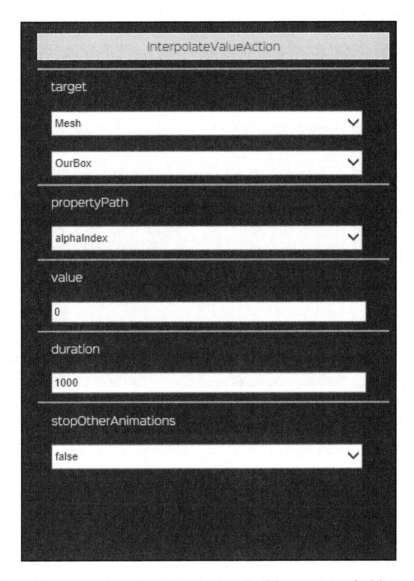

The equivalent of the `.then` function in the Actions Builder consists of adding a child action to an action.

Let's also add a condition to the graph and a child action of the interpolate value action (equivalent to .then). As for triggers and actions, *drag'n'drop* a value condition (BABYLON.ValueCondition) on the interpolate value action, as shown in the following screenshot:

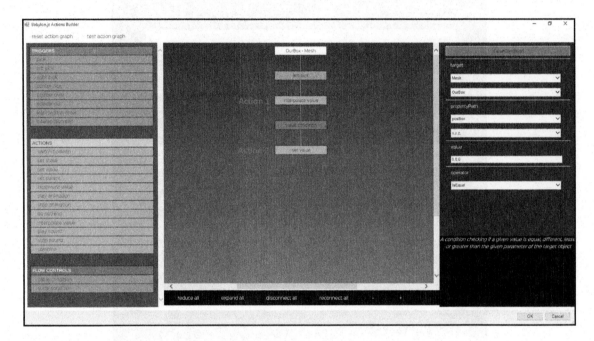

Here, Action 1 will be executed when the user left-clicks on the mesh. Once Action 1 is executed, Action 2 is executed only if the value condition returns true.

Managing multiple pipelines

Using TypeScript, you can add multiple branches of actions to your object by calling the .registerAction function in the ActionManager object. With the Actions Builder, you can simply add another trigger that will handle a new graph of actions, as shown in the following screenshot:

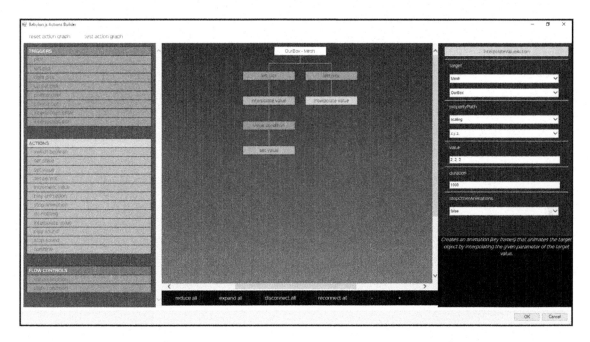

With this configuration, the first actions of each trigger will be executed simultaneously, except if there are conditions and if the condition of an action returns false.

Summary

You are now able to create actions in your projects and save a lot of lines of code. You know how to use the BABYLON.ActionManager class, how to add actions, the different triggers, and how to control the graph using conditions. You are also able to work with artists and 3ds Max using the Actions Builder and save more lines of code.

In the next chapter, let's concentrate on the rendering part using post-processes (effects). It'll be an occasion to introduce the notion of HDR, SSAO, blurring, blooming, and so on. It's one of the favorite parts of the 3D developers to create special effects such as post-processes.

8

Add Rendering Effects Using Built-in Post-processes

Remember Chapter 4, *Using Materials to Customize 3D Objects Appearance*, about materials? Behind the materials are GPU programs called **shaders**. Shaders are a combination of two linked programs: the vertex shader and the pixel shader. The vertex shader works on vertices (transforms their 3D positions to 2D positions on the screen), while the pixel shader works on pixels (determines the final color of each pixel). Here, you can see the post-processes to be only a pixel shader since the vertex shader is the same for all.

Finally, the post-processes tend to create effects only in the view space. In other words, the post-processes are never applied to objects such as meshes, they are applied only to the camera itself. In this chapter, we will cover the following topics:

- Using post-processes with Babylon.js
- Using post-process rendering pipelines with Babylon.js
- Discussing the built-in post-processes

Using post-processes with Babylon.js

Fortunately, you'll not have to create post-processes yourself, even if you can do it with Babylon.js. There are post-processes already available in Babylon.js and in most cases, available by writing only a line of code!

Starting with your first post-process

With the post-processes available in Babylon.js, you can create blur, bloom, HDR, SSAO, volumetric light post-processes, and so on.

Let's start with the following scene:

For the first example, let's create a vertical blur post-process using the built-in post-processes. The blur post-process is available by creating a new instance of the BABYLON.BlurPostProcess class, as follows:

```
var blurV = new BABYLON.BlurPostProcess(
  "blurV", // Name of the post-process
  new BABYLON.Vector2(0, 1), // Direction of the blur (vertical)
  4, // The blur width
  0.5, // The ratio of the post-process
  camera // The camera to attach to
);
```

The result is as shown in the following screenshot:

The majority of post-processes available in Babylon.js will have the same parameters as shown in the following:

- **Name**: This is the name of the post-process.
- **Ratio**: This is the ratio of the post-process in the [0, 1] interval. The ratio is used to calculate the post-process in a lower resolution in order to save performances. In other words, with a ratio of 0.5, the post-process will be applied to the canvas resolution divided by 2.
- **Camera**: The post-processes are applied on the cameras. Then, you just have to provide the camera reference and the post-process's constructors attaches itself to the camera.

For another example, let's create a black and white post-process that will make the scene entirely black and white, as follows:

```
var bw = new BABYLON.BlackAndWhitePostProcess(
  "blackAndWhite", // name of the post-process
  1.0, // ratio of 1.0, keep the full resolution
  camera // the camera to attach to
);
```

The following screenshot displays the result:

Chaining post-processes

With Babylon.js, you can chain post-processes. This means that for a post-process, the previous post-process will be used as a reference. For example, two blur post-processes can be used to blur the scene horizontally and vertically; the first post-process blurs the scene horizontally and the second uses the horizontal blur post-process to blur the scene vertically.

Let's create the first post-process that is the horizontal blur post-process:

```
var blurH = new BABYLON.BlurPostProcess(
    "blurH",
    new BABYLON.Vector2(1, 0),
    8,
    0.5,
    camera
);
```

Now, let's create the vertical blur post-process after the horizontal blur post-process, as follows:

```
var blurV = new BABYLON.BlurPostProcess(
  "blurV",
  new BABYLON.Vector2(0, 1),
  8,
  0.5,
  camera
);
```

Finally, why not add the `black and white` post-process, as shown in the following:

```
var bw = new BABYLON.BlackAndWhitePostProcess("bw", 1.0, camera);
```

The final result is displayed in the following screenshot:

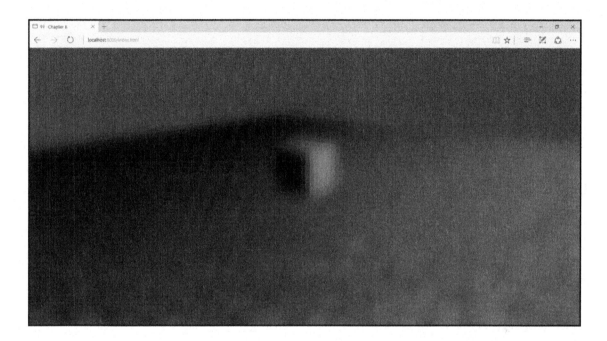

Removing and retrieving post-processes

To remove a post-process from the camera, you can simply call the `.dispose` function on a post-process. The dispose function removes the internal resources and detaches the post-process from the camera.

For example, consider the following with the previous chained post-processes:

```
blurH.dispose();
blurV.dispose();
bw.dispose();
```

Conversely, you can detach and attach a post-process from/to a camera without removing the internal resources. Simply, call the `.attachPostProcess` or `.detachPostProcess` functions on a camera. Consider the following example:

```
camera.detachPostProcess(blurH); // Detach
camera.attachPostProcess(blurH); // Re-attach the post-process
```

To retrieve the available post-processes, you can access the `._postProcesses` property of a camera. Consider the following example:

```
for (var i=0; i < camera._postProcesses.length; i++) {
  console.log(camera._postProcesses[i].name);
}
```

Using post-process rendering pipelines with Babylon.js

Now, you are able to create post-processes and attach them to a camera. The problem is that if you manage multiple cameras in your project, then you'll have to dispose or detach post-processes in order to reattach them to a new camera. To facilitate the task, you can use the rendering pipelines. In other words, you can see a rendering pipeline as a list of post-processes, which you can attach to multiple cameras.

Create a rendering pipeline

The steps consist on creating a pipeline reference, adding the pipeline to the scene, and attaching the pipeline to the cameras.

Create a rendering pipeline, as follows:

```
var pipeline = new BABYLON.PostProcessRenderPipeline(
  engine, // The Babylon.js engine
  "renderingPipeline" // The name of the rendering pipeline
);
```

Once the pipeline has been created, add it to the post-process render pipeline manager of the scene (referenced by the engine that you passed as an argument to the rendering pipeline's constructor), as follows:

```
scene.postProcessRenderPipelineManager.addPipeline(pipeline);
```

Once the pipeline is added to the post-process render pipeline manager, you are able to add the effects. The process consists of adding a new `BABYLON.PostProcessRenderEffect` object to the pipeline by calling the `.addEffect` method to the pipeline, as shown in the following snippet:

```
// Create the post-process (horizontal blur)
var blurH = new BABYLON.BlurPostProcess(
  "blurH",
  new BABYLON.Vector2(1, 0), 8, 0.5,
```

```
    null, // The camera is null
    null, // Keep the bilinear filter as default
    engine // Because the camera is null, we must provide the engine
);
// Create the render effect
var blurHEffect = new BABYLON.PostProcessRenderEffect(
    engine, // The Babylon.js engine
    "blurHEffect", // The name of the post-process render effect
    () => { // The function that returns the wanted post-process
        return blurH;
    }
);
// Add the render effect to the pipeline
pipeline.addEffect(blurHEffect);
```

As you can see, the method to construct the post-processes must be changed. Now, the post-processes will not take any camera as an argument since they are not applied to a specific camera. This is the reason why we must provide all the arguments, such as the filter type (bilinear as default, then can be null) and the engine. This method is the same for all the post-processes, you can easily add post-process render effects to the pipeline, as follows:

```
var blurH = new BABYLON.BlurPostProcess(..);
var blurV = new BABYLON.BlurPostProcess(..);
var bw = new BABYLON.BlackAndWhitePostProcess(..);
// The horizontal blur post-process render effect
var blurHEffect = new BABYLON.PostProcessRenderEffect(
    engine, // The Babylon.js engine
    "blurHEffect",
    () => {
        return blurH;
    }
);
// The vertical blur post-process render effect
var blurVEffect = new BABYLON.PostProcessRenderEffect(
    engine, // The Babylon.js engine
    "blurVEffect",
    () => {
        return blurV;
    }
);
// The black and white post-process render effect
var bwEffect = new BABYLON.PostProcessRenderEffect(
    engine,
    "bwEffect",
    () => {
        return bw;
    }
);
```

```
// And finally add the render effects to the pipeline by
// following the desired order
pipeline.addEffect(blurHEffect);
pipeline.addEffect(blurVEffect);
pipeline.addEffect(bwEffect);
```

Finally, let's attach the pipeline to a camera or a list of cameras. The post-process will now be applied to the cameras, as shown in the following snippet:

```
scene.postProcessRenderPipelineManager.attachCamerasToRenderPipeline(
    "renderingPipeline", // The name of the pipeline to attach
    camera // the camera to attach to. Can be an array of cameras
);
```

You can also detach the pipeline from a camera or a list of cameras, as follows:

```
scene.postProcessRenderPipelineManager.detachCamerasFromRenderPipeline(
    "renderingPipeline", // The name of the pipeline to detach
    camera // the camera to detach. Can be an array of cameras
);
```

The result looks exactly the same; however, now it's easier to share the post-processes among your multiple cameras, as shown in the following screenshot:

Enabling and disabling effects in pipeline

Another particularity of the post-process render pipelines is the possibility of disabling and enabling effects, a useful feature that allows you to highly debug the rendering part of your project.

Consider that, in your project, you can switch between two cameras (`scene.activeCamera = theNewCamera`). The first camera is blurred and the second is blurred and `black and white`. The goal is that the two cameras can share the same post-process render pipeline reference, except that the first camera must have the `black and white` post-process disabled.

To disable an effect in a render pipeline, you can call the `.disableEffectInPipeline` method on the post-process render pipeline manager of your scene. The only parameters needed are the pipeline's name, the effect's name, and the camera that will no longer have the post-process enabled. If we take the previous example, let's deactivate the `black and white` post-process, as follows:

```
scene.postProcessRenderPipelineManager.disableEffectInPipeline(
    "renderingPipeline", // The name of the render pipeline
    "bwEffect", // The name of the "black and white" effect to disable
    camera // The camera attached to the pipeline
);
```

In other words, this method allows you to deactivate a render effect only for the camera passed as an argument.

Conversely, at any time, you can enable a render effect that is previously disabled by calling the `.enableEffectInPipeline` method on the post-process render pipeline manager of your scene. Let's enable the `black and white` render effect, as shown in the following:

```
scene.postProcessRenderPipelineManager.enableEffectInPipeline(
    "renderingPipeline", // The name of the render pipeline
    "bwEffect", // The name of the "black and white" effect to enable
    camera // The camera attached to the pipeline
);
```

The built-in post-processes

Let's start with the most interesting part of this chapter; the use of the built-in post-processes in Babylon.js. There are several post-processes that can beautify your scenes only though the use of the following elements:

- **Volumetric light scattering**: This shows how to easily scatter the light rays of a given light source, such as a sun or a moon.
- **SSAO rendering pipeline**: Screen-Space Ambient Occlusion. In other words, this rendering pipeline tends to approximate the ambient occlusion of a scene for more realism, only using a post-process.
- **HDR rendering pipeline**: High Dynamic Range rendering. This rendering pipeline is directly related to the lighting in the scene and tends to simulate the way retinas work in the real world.

Volumetric Light Scattering post-process

Let's start this fun part with the **Volumetric Light Scattering (VLS)** post-process. The VLS post-process tends to simulate the scattering of light rays from a light source according to the obstacles between the light and the camera.

Let's take the following original scene:

The VLS post-process takes a mesh that will represent the light color as an argument. In fact, the light source isn't really a light (BABYLON.Light), but a mesh with a material configured to simulate the light's color by a diffuse texture or color.

Let's consider, for example, a white sun represented by a billboard. With the VLS post-process, the result looks similar to the following screenshot:

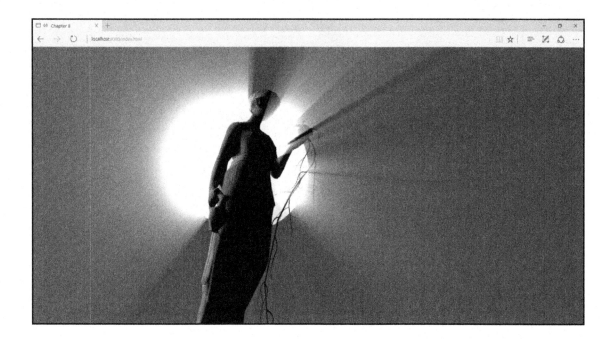

The scene, without the post-process, looks similar to the following screenshot:

The rounded white mesh is, in fact, a plane with a diffuse texture that contains alpha. The diffuse texture can be found in the example files and is named `sun.png`.

Let's create the VLS post-process, as follows:

```
var vls = new BABYLON.VolumetricLightScatteringPostProcess(
  "vls", // The name of the post-process
  1.O, // The ratio of the post-process
  camera, // The camera to attach to
  null, // The mesh used as light source
  100 // Number of samples. Means the quality of the post-process
);
```

In the VLS constructor, if the mesh parameter is null, the post-process creates a default mesh that is a plane rendered as a billboard. At any time, if you want, you can access the method as shown in the following:

```
BABYLON.VolumetricLightScatteringPostProcess.CreateDefaultMesh(
  "vlsMesh", // The name of the billboard plane mesh
  scene // The scene where to add the billboard plane mesh
);
```

For example, the mansion scene of Babylon.js used the VLS post-process to scatter the moon's light rays. The result was the following image:

The method is pretty simple, they just got the moon's mesh reference and created the VLS post-process by passing the moon's mesh reference as parameter, as follows:

```
var moon = scene.getMeshByName("moon");
var vls = new BABYLON.VolumetricLightScatteringPostProcess(
  "vls", // The name of the post-process
  1.0, // The ratio of the post-process
  camera, // The camera to attach to
  moon, // The mesh used as light source
  75 // Number of samples. Means the quality of the post-process
);
```

The number of samples is typically in the [30, 100] interval and defines the quality of the post-process's result. In the mansion scene of Babylon.js, the number of samples was set to 65 in order to save the performance due to the pretty large and really nice scene that was already rendered by the engine.

To save more performance, the ratio of the post-process can be more customized. In fact, the VLS post-process uses an internal pass that renders the scene in a texture (Render Target Texture) to create the scattering of light rays. You can easily configure the internal pass in order to render in a lower resolution. Simply pass an object as an argument for the ratio, as shown in the following snippet:

```
var ratio = {
  passRatio: 0.25, // Ratio of the internal pass. Render in a texture
  // with a size divided per 4
  postProcessRatio: 1.0 // Ratio of the post-process
};
var vls = new BABYLON.VolumetricLightScatteringPostProcess(
  "vls", // The name of the post-process
  ratio, // The ratio object
  camera, // The camera to attach to
  moon, // The mesh used as light source
  100 // Number of samples. Means the quality of the post-process
);
```

You can also customize the parameters related to the VLS post-process itself.

The exposure controls the overall intensity of the effect (default 0.3), as follows:

```
vls.exposure = 0.7; // Exaggerated value
```

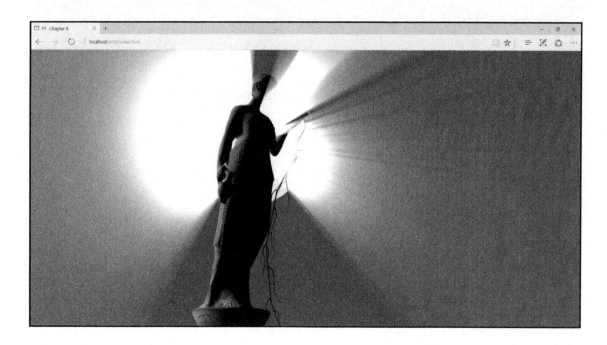

The decay dissipates each sample's contribution (default `0.96815`), as shown in the following code:

```
vls.decay = 0.9;
```

The weight controls the overall intensity of each sample (default 0.58767), as shown in the following code:

```
vls.weight = 0.8;
```

The density controls the density of each sample (default 0.926), as shown in the following code:

```
vls.density = 0.7;
```

To give you an order, the mansion scene of Babylon.js was configured as follows:

```
var moon = scene.getMeshByName("Moon");
var vls = new BABYLON.VolumetricLightScatteringPostProcess(
  "vls",
  1.0,
  scene.activeCamera,
  moon,
  65,
);
vls.exposure = 0.15;
vls.weight = 0.54;
```

SSAO rendering pipeline

The SSAO effect is a rendering pipeline as it counts the following five post-processes:

- Pass post-process (saves the scene in a texture)
- SSAO post-process
- Horizontal blur post-process
- Vertical blur post-process

- Combine post-process

The SSAO is famous as it computes the ambient occlusion only using the screen space (post-process) in contrast with the more classical methods that require the 3D artists to calculate the ambient occlusion in their textures. Finally, the SSAO is a good way to save textures and the weight of your projects (no more textures required).

Let's see the SSAO effect in this scene, the scene without SSAO, the scene with SSAO, and finally the scene with only SSAO enabled:

The result is particularly discreet; however, it can highly add realism to your scenes. The ambient occlusion is the way to represent the capacity of the light rays to access the objects at its different points, or specifically with SSAO, the light rays that cannot access the objects at its different points.

At a various point of view, the effect can be easily perceived, as shown in the following images:

The SSAO is a render pipeline and can be easily created, as follows:

```
var ssao = new BABYLON.SSAORenderingPipeline(
  "ssao", // The name of the render pipeline
  scene, // The scene where to add the render pipeline
```

```
    1.0 // The ratio of SSAO post-process
  );
  // Attach the render pipeline to your camera
  scene.postProcessRenderPipelineManager.attachCamerasToRenderPipeline(
    "ssao", // Name of the render pipeline
    camera // The camera to attach to
  );
```

That's all. Fortunately, the SSAO, the horizontal, and the vertical blur post-processes can be done at a lower resolution than the screen size. As for the VLS post-process, you can pass an object for the ratio parameter, as follows:

```
var ratio = {
  ssaoRatio: 0.25, // Size divided per 4, saves a lot of performances!
  combineRatio: 1.0 // The final output that mixes SSAO with the scene
};
var ssao = new BABYLON.SSAORenderingPipeline(
  "ssao", // The name of the render pipeline
  scene, // The scene where to add the render pipeline
  ratio // The ratio of SSAO post-process
);
```

In each scene's function, you may have to configure the SSAO to render perfectly. There are several parameters that you can customize, as follows:

- The total strength: This controls the overall intensity of the effect (default 1.0).
  The `.totalStrength` property is rarely or slightly modified as it can create
  some artifacts.
- The radius: This represents the radius around the analyzed pixel by the SSAO
  (default 0.0002). To calculate the **Ambient** Occlusion (**AO**) of the current pixel,
  the SSAO effect computes 16 samples around the current pixel in the
  specified `.radius` property.
- The area: The `.area` (default 0.0075) property is used to interpolate the SSAO
  samples based on the occlusion difference of each pixel. In other words, the area
  is used to smooth the ambient occlusion of each sample of each pixel. Take a look
  at the following example of a smooth function base on a line (from Wikipedia):

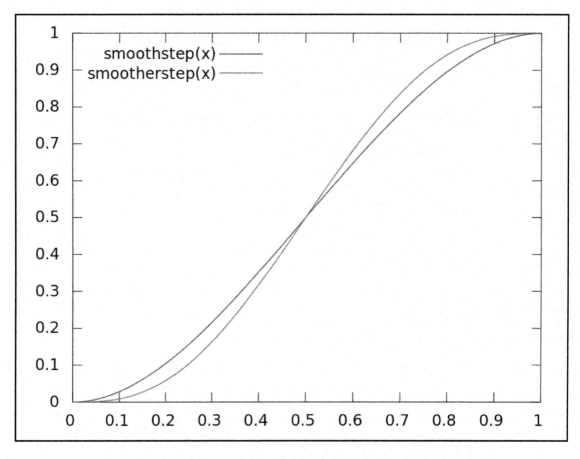

In the example files, you can press the **2** key to disable SSAO, **1** to enable SSAO, and **3** to only draw the SSAO pass. The results (in order) are shown in the following images:

HDR rendering pipeline

The **High Dynamic Range** (**HDR**) was a buzzword for a long time. This concept, particularly interesting, tends to simulate how the retinas operate in the real world. It includes the adaptation of luminosity (glaring) and the luminosity artifacts on the highlighted surfaces of an object.

To understand the effect of glare, imagine that you are in a totally dark room. Suddenly, someone turns the light on; the necessary time for your eye to adapt to the luminosity (bloomed and blurred) represents the glare effect.

Let's compare the same scene with and without the HDR render pipeline enabled (HDR will adapt the luminosity and create artifacts on the highlighted zones), as shown in the following images:

To create an HDR render pipeline, the process is the same as the SSAO render pipeline, as follows:

```
var hdr = new BABYLON.HDRRenderingPipeline(
    "hdr", // The name of the render pipeline
    scene, // The scene where to add the render pipeline
    1.0, // ratio of the render pipeline. Here, the ratio is a number
);
```

```
// Finally, attach the render pipeline to a camera
scene.postProcessRenderPipelineManager.attachCamerasToRenderPipeline(
  "hdr", // The name of the render pipeline
  camera // The camera to attach to
);
```

The HDR rendering pipeline can be highly customized as you can customize the minimum luminosity required to create the artifacts, create the blur effect that creates the artifacts, the speed of retina adaptation of luminosity, and so on.

The exposure (`hdr.exposure`) controls the overall luminosity of the scene (default 1.0), as shown in the following:

```
hdr.exposure = 1.8;
```

The bright threshold (`hdr.brightThreshold`) controls the minimum luminance required to create the artifacts (default `0.8`), as shown in the following:

```
hdr.brightThreshold = 0.2;
```

The minimum luminance (`hdr.minimumLuminance`) represents the retina adaptation in the darker zones (default `1.0`). The smaller the value (`>= 0.0`), the more highlighted the scene is, as shown in the following:

```
hdr.minimumLuminance = 0.0;
```

The luminance decrease rate (`hdr.luminanceDecreaseRate`) and luminance increase rate (hdr.luminanceIncreaserate) represent the speed of retina adaptation to the luminosity (default 0.5 for both). The higher the value, the quicker the adaptation. In most cases, the value is between 0.5 and 1.0.

The Gaussian blur multiplier (hdr.gaussMultiplier) intensifies the blur width (default 4). It works the .blurWidth property of BABYLON.BlurPostProcess, as shown in the following:

```
hdr.gaussMultiplier = 8;
```

The Gaussian coefficient (hdr.gaussCoeff) controls the overall Gaussian blur effect (default 0.3). In fact, the output of the Gaussian blur is *output * gaussCoeff*, as shown in the following:

```
hdr.gaussCoeff = 0.8;
```

The Gaussian standard deviaition (`hdr.gaussStandDev`) controls the overall blur intensity of the effect (default 0.8), as shown in the following:

```
hdr.gaussStandDev = 0.2;
```

The `.gausCoeff` and `.gaussStandDev` properties are linked together. They must be equilibrated relative to each other. To give you an order, the following scene is configured:

```
var hdr = new BABYLON.HDRRenderingPipeline("hdr", scene, 1.0);
hdr.brightThreshold = 0.5;
hdr.gaussCoeff = 0.7;
hdr.gaussMean = 1.0;
hdr.gaussStandDev = 7.5;
hdr.minimumLuminance = 0.7;
hdr.luminanceDecreaseRate = 1.0;
hdr.luminanceIncreaserate = 1.0;
hdr.exposure = 1.3;
hdr.gaussMultiplier = 4;
```

It looks like the following:

In most cases, in a highlighted scene, following the Gaussian Blur equations with the implementation of HDR in Babylon.js, the Gaussian Standard Deviation equals *10.0 * Gaussian Coefficient.*

Summary

In this chapter, you learned how to beautify your scenes using only post-processes. The Mansion demo on the Babylon.js home page showed a great usage of the Volumetric Light Scattering post-process. Unfortunately, none of the post-processes are available on phones due to hardware limitations. Even if the post-process is not supported on mobiles, your projects will still run without the post-process being rendered. The power of Babylon.js resides in the fact that it works on all devices. Even if a feature is not supported on a device, the feature will simply be disabled.

In the next chapter, let's end this with animations. The Babylon.js framework allows creating and managing animations. These animations will allow you to animate characters, objects, and more with the help of the framework and 3D artists!

9
Create and Play Animations

In the previous chapters, you learned everything that is required to create cool, beautiful, and complete 3D applications. This is the last chapter and the last thing that you need to learn is how to animate objects in your scene. Then, finally, you will get a fully dynamic scene.

The Babylon.js framework provides a way to create animations without managing them with code. For example, you want to create a rotation animation that will affect five objects (nodes) in your scene; Babylon.js will allow you to create an animation object that you can share easily between your five nodes. In this chapter, we'll cover the following topics:

- Creating animations using Babylon.js
- Smooth animations using easing functions
- Importing and managing animated models

Creating animations using Babylon.js

For this first topic, let's discuss how to simply animate a box with code and how to create an animation using the Babylon.js tools such as the `BABYLON.Animation` class. You'll quickly understand the importance of using the provided tools instead of handling animations with code.

Animating an object with code

Let's start with the following scene (a plane and a box):

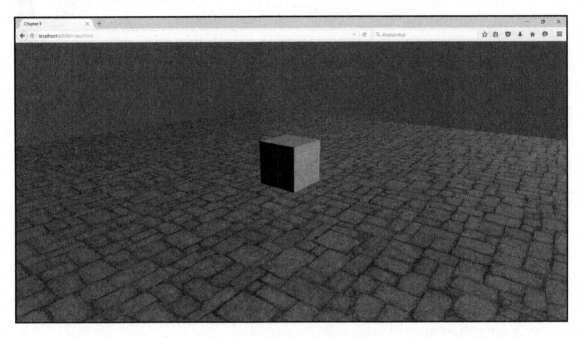

Let's animate the box to turn around its center (x = 0, y = 0, and z = 0). The process should be to increment a value (angle) in time and set the new position of the box.

Typically, (*x = Radius*Cos(angle), y = 0*, and *z = Radius*Sin(angle)*).

To perform this action, you can call a .registerBeforeRender function on the scene. This function takes an anonymous function as the parameter and this anonymous function will be automatically called for every frame, as follows:

```
var angle = 0.0;
var radius = 10.0;
scene.registerBeforeRender(() => {
  angle += 0.01; // Increment the angle
  // Set the new position of the box
  box.position.x = radius * Math.cos(angle);
  box.position.z = radius * Math.sin(angle);
});
```

This function is pretty simple; however, it is applied only to the box. What if you want to animate another object by sharing the same code? The solution is simple; just pass the node as a parameter to a function that will register a new function at each call before render, as follows:

```
var createAnimation = function(node) {
  var angle = 0.0;
  var radius = 10.0;
  scene.registerBeforeRender(() => {
    angle += 0.01; // Increment the angle
    // Set the new position of the box
    node.position.x = radius * Math.cos(angle);
    node.position.z = radius * Math.sin(angle);
  });
}
```

As you can see, it is not necessarily a problem to manage the animations through code. The real problem occurs when you have to synchronize the animation with time (manage the speed of animation), stop or pause animations, and so on. These functions require you to create a complete manager and it is not necessary what you want to do.

The next sub-topic will show you how to use the animation manager of Babylon.js and don't worry about the time, stop and pause functions, and so on.

Using the animation manager of Babylon.js

Let's take the same scene and create a simple animation only using the animation manager of Babylon.js. You need to understand only one thing: the frame keys of an animation.

To create an animation, just use the BABYLON.Animation class and attach it to a node (or several nodes). The BABYLON.Animation class isn't difficult to understand, it takes a name, a property to animate on a node (and not necessarily a property of a node), number of frames per second, data type, and loop mode, as shown in the following snippet:

```
var simpleAnimation = new BABYLON.Animation(
  "simpleAnimation", // Name of the animation
  "rotation", // The property to modify (node.rotation)
  1, // Frames per second
  BABYLON.Animation.ANIMATIONTYPE_VECTOR3, // The type of property
  BABYLON.Animation.ANIMATIONLOOPMODE_CYCLE // The loop mode
);
```

The rotation parameter says that the animation manager will animate the .rotation property of the object attached to the animation. A rotation is of the BABYLON.Vector3 type, this is the reason why the data type is

`BABYLON.Animation.ANIMATIONTYPE_VECTOR3`. Finally, we want the animation to loop.

According to the property you are animating (*rotation* in the previous example that is a `BABYLON.Vector3` object), you have to provide a valid data type which can be one of the following:

- `ANIMATIONTYPE_FLOAT`: When the property is of the `float` type.
- `ANIMATIONTYPE_VECTOR2`: When the property is of the `BABYLON.Vector2` type.
- `ANIMATIONTYPE_VECTOR3`: When the property is of the `BABYLON.Vector3` type.
- `ANIMATIONTYPE_QUATERNION`: When the property is of the `BABYLON.Quaternion` type. A mathematical object that can be used to represent the rotation of a node (`node.rotationQuaternion`)
- `ANIMATIONTYPE_MATRIX`: When the property is of the `BABYLON.Matrix` type.
- `ANIMATIONTYPE_COLOR3`: When the property is of the `BABYLON.Color3` type.

In this case, we use the `Vector3` data type as the `.rotation` property is `BABYLON.Vector3`.

The next step consists of creating an array of keys. The keys (or key frames) represent the state of the animated property at specific frames. In the previously created animation, the number of frames per second was set to `1`. Then, each second, a key, in the array of keys, is reached. The keys of an animation is simply an array of objects, objects each composed of two properties: the frame number and, according to the animated property, the associated value (of type `float`, `BABYLON.Vector2`, or `BABYLON.Vector3`, and so on.), as follows:

```
{
    frame: number;
    value: any;
}
```

Let's create two keys that will translate the box from the position (x = 0, y = 2.5, and z = 0) to (x = 10, y = 10, and z = 10) at frame 20, as follows:

```
var keys = [
{
  frame: 0,
  value: new BABYLON.Vector3(0, 0, 0)
},
{
  frame: 20,
  value: new BABYLON.Vector3(10, 10, 10)
}
];
```

If the number of frames per second is set to 1, the second key (`frame = 20`) means that the box position will be at (`x = 10, y = 10, and z = 10`) 20 seconds later.

Let's set the keys for the `simpleAnimation` animation manager, as follows:

```
simpleAnimation.setKeys(keys);
```

Finally, let's attach the animation manager to the box and start the animation in the scene, as follows:

```
// Add animation to the box
// Every BABYLON.Node object has the ".animations" property
box.animations.push(simpleAnimation);
// Start animation
scene.beginAnimation(
  box, // Start animation(s) of the box
  0, // Start key. Here 0
  20, // End key. Here 20
  true, // Loop the animation
  1, // Speed ratio. Controls the speed of animation
  () => { // Callback. Called when animation finished
    console.log("Finished");
  }
);
```

The result looks similar to the following at the beginning:

Finally, once the animation has finished, the result looks like:

To reproduce the previous example (the box that turns around the center), the solution is pretty simple; just add 360 keys that represent every degree of a circle, as follows:

```
// Create animation
var complexAnimation = new BABYLON.Animation(
  "boxAnimationComplex",
  "position",
  60, // 60 frames per second
  BABYLON.Animation.ANIMATIONTYPE_VECTOR3,
  BABYLON.Animation.ANIMATIONLOOPMODE_CYCLE
);
// Create keys
var complexKeys = [];
for (var i=0; i < 360; i++) {
  // Transform the degrees into radians
  var angle = BABYLON.Tools.ToRadians(i);
  complexKeys.push({
    frame: i,
    value: new BABYLON.Vector3(10 * Math.cos(angle),
    2.5,
    10 * Math.sin(angle))
  });
}
// Set the keys
```

```
complexAnimation.setKeys(complexKeys);
// Finally run the animation(s)
scene.beginAnimation(this._box, 0, 360, false, 1.0, () => {
  console.log("Animation Finished");
});
```

To control your animations (start, pause, restart, and stop), the `.beginAnimation` function returns an object of the `BABYLON.Animatable` type. The returned object is created on the fly and allows you to control your animations. Let's consider the same example as earlier:

```
var anim = scene.beginAnimation(this._box, 0, 360, false, 1.0, () => {
  console.log("Animation Finished");
});
// Pause animation
anim.pause();
// Start the animation (when stopped or paused)
anim.start();
// Restart animation
anim.restart();
// Stop animation
anim.stop();
// Go to a specific frame
anim.goToFrame(180);
```

Create a simple animation

The first example, with only two frames, can be heavy as I know that you'll quickly create a helper, once and for all. Babylon.js thought about this and provides a static `CreateAndStartAnimation` function that creates two frames and starts the animation for you. Let's create the same animation only using the following function:

```
var anim: BABYLON.Animation = BABYLON.Animation.CreateAndStartAnimation(
  "quickAnimation", // name of the animation
  box, // The mesh to animate
  "position", // The property to animate
  1, // frames per second
  20, // number of frames of the animation
  new BABYLON.Vector3(0, 0, 0), // The start value
  new BABYLON.Vector3(10, 10, 10), // The end value
  BABYLON.Animation.ANIMATIONLOOPMODE_CYCLE // The loop mode
);
```

As you can guess, this method is used by Babylon.js to create `BABYLON.InterpolateValueAction` (Chapter 7, *Defining Actions on Objects*).

Managing events

An advanced use of the Babylon.js animations is to call a function when a specific frame is reached. The BABYLON.AnimationEvent class exists to allow you to attach one or more events to a specific frame. For example, consider the previous example (complexAnimation), as follows:

```
var event = new BABYLON.AnimationEvent(
  180, // The frame when the callback will be called
  () => { // The function executed when the current frame is 180
    console.log("My event was called!");
  },
  false // Only once? False, we want to call the callback every ti  me//
the frame is reached
);
// Add the event to the animation
complexAnimation.addEvent(event);
```

Using easing functions to smooth animations

One of the advanced features of the Babylon.js animations management is to use easing functions to smooth well and add behaviors to your animations.

To take a quick look at the appearance of the easing functions (we do not necessarily remember every type of easing functions), you should follow this link (http://easings.net/en).

Applying an easing function to an animation

To apply an easing function to an animation, the method only consists of customizing an already created animation. You'll just have to call the .setEasingFunction method for an animation with an easing function as the parameter.

The available easing functions are (with the associated curve in time) as shown in the following:

* Circle ease: BABYLON.CircleEase()

- Back ease: `BABYLON.BackEase(amplitude)`

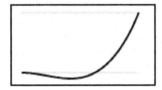

- Bounce ease: `BABYLON.BounceEase(bounces, bounciness)`

- Cubic ease: `BABYLON.CubicEase()`

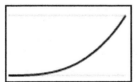

- **Elastic ease:** `BABYLON.ElasticEase(oscillations, springiness)`

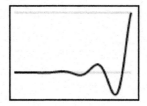

- **Exponential ease:** `BABYLON.ExponentialEase(exponent)`

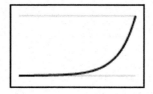

- **Quadratic ease:** `BABYLON.QuadraticEase()`

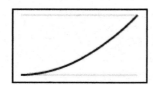

- **Quartic ease:** `BABYLON.QuarticEase()`

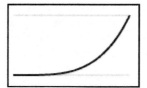

- Quintic ease: `BABYLON.QuinticEase()`

- Sine ease: `BABYLON.SineEase()`

Let's start with the following simple example (animate the .x property of the box's rotation using a circle easing function):

```
// Create and set easing function (circle ease)
var ease = new BABYLON.CircleEase();
easingAnimation.setEasingFunction(ease);
```

That's all, the animation will now follow the formula of the circle easing function, as shown in the following:

```
// Create animation
var easingAnimation = new BABYLON.Animation(
  "easingAnimation",
  "rotation.x", // Modify the .x property of rotation
  10, // 10 frames per second
  BABYLON.Animation.ANIMATIONTYPE_VECTOR3,
  BABYLON.Animation.ANIMATIONLOOPMODE_CYCLE
);
// Create keys
var simpleKeys = [
  {
    frame: 0,
    value: 0
  },
  {
    frame: 20,
    value: Math.PI
```

```
      },
      {
        frame: 40,
        value: 0
      }
    ];
    // Set keys
    easingAnimation.setKeys(simpleKeys);
    // Push animation
    this._box.animations.push(easingAnimation);
    // Create and set easing function (circle ease)
    var ease = new BABYLON.CircleEase();
    easingAnimation.setEasingFunction(ease);
    // Finally, start the animation(s) of the box
    this._scene.beginAnimation(box, 0, 40, true, 1.0, () => {
      console.log("Animation Finished");
    });
```

As it is hard to represent an animation by taking screenshots, you can try the different easing functions by yourself. The method is the same for all the easing functions, except that several easing function constructors will need some arguments for more customization.

Now, let's modify the behavior of the easing function. An easing function consists of modes, as shown in the following:

- `In`, when the animation starts
  (enters): `BABYLON.EasingFunction.EASINGMODE_EASEIN`
- `Out`, when the animation is completed
  (exits): `BABYLON.EasingFunction.EASINGMODE_EASEOUT`
- `In` & `Out`, when the animation starts and finishes (both enter and exit): `BABYLON.EasingFunction.EASINGMODE_EASEINOUT`

By default, the easing mode is set to `In` (`BABYLON.EasingFunction.EASINGMODE_EASEIN`). The website `http://easings.net/en` shows exactly how the easing functions look in these three modes.

To specify the easing mode, just call the `.setEasingMode` method on an animation, as follows:

```
// Create and set easing function (circle ease)
var ease = new BABYLON.CircleEase();
ease.setEasingMode(BABYLON.EasingFunction.EASINGMODE_EASEINOUT);
easingAnimation.setEasingFunction(ease);
```

Creating your own easing function

For the last sub-topic about easing functions, let's discuss how to create your own easing function if it is not available in Babylon.js. The process is really simple (except the possible difficult mathematical formula(s) associated with your easing function).

Just create a class that inherits from the `BABYLON.EasingFunction` class that implements the `BABYLON.IEasingFunction` interface. The only thing to do is to implement the `.easeInCore(gradient: number)` function that takes the interpolated value as the parameter.

Let's create an example with a Power easing function, as follows:

```
export class PowerEase extends BABYLON.EasingFunction
{
  constructor(public power: number = 2) {
    // Call constructor of BABYLON.EasingFunction
    super();
  }
  public easeInCore(gradient: number): number {
    var y = Math.max(0.0, this.power);
    return Math.pow(gradient, y);
  }
}
Somewhere in your code:
// Create and set easing function (circle ease)
var customEase = new BABYLON.PowerEase(4);
customEase.setEasingMode(BABYLON.EasingFunction.EASINGMODE_EASEINOUT);
easingAnimation.setEasingFunction(customEase);
```

Importing and managing animated models

To finish this chapter with a cool demo, let's discuss how to animate characters or 3D models, in general.

How 3D animated models work

If you remember, each vertex of a 3D model is computed to be projected on the screen by a vertex shader. In fact, the animated 3D models (such as a character) are also animated with the associated hierarchy of bones (the hierarchy is called **Skeleton**). Animated 3D models are also called **Skinned Meshes**. In 3D engines, the bones are invisible nodes that are animated (`BABYLON.Animation`) to be sent to the vertex shader associated with the 3D model. In other words, the transformation of each bone is sent to the vertex shader and is applied to the associated vertices.

To go further in the theory, the vertex shader contains the following two additional buffers:

- The bones' matrices weights (Vector4, represents the *intensity* of the influence of each bone on the current vertex).
- The bones' matrices indices (Vector4, until four bone influences per vertex) work like the indices buffer, but for bones. In other words, for each vertex, which bones influence the vertex (indices in the array of bones' transformations).

 Note: The common buffers for static 3D models are the positions (required), indices (required), normals (not required), UVs (texture coordinates, not required), and colors (not required).

Finally, for each vertex, the formula (in GLSL) is as follows:

```
uniform mat4 bones[NUMBER_OF_BONES]; // Sent by Babylon.js
mat4 boneTransform1 = bones[matricesIndices[0]] * matricesWeights[0];
mat4 boneTransform2 = bones[matricesIndices[1]] * matricesWeights[1];
mat4 boneTransform3 = bones[matricesIndices[2]] * matricesWeights[2];
mat4 boneTransform4 = bones[matricesIndices[3]] * matricesWeights[3];
mat4 finalTransform = transformedVertex * (
  boneTransform1 + boneTransform2 +
    boneTransform3 + boneTransform4
);
```

When artists export their 3D models (animated with the tools provided by the modeling software), the Babylon.js exporters (3ds Max and Blender) explicitly write the bones' weights' buffers and the bones' matrices indices buffers in the exported file, which arrays of numbers. In conclusion, for animated 3D models, you don't have to specify the animations through code, the exporters can do everything for you. Let's wait until the next sub-topic to learn how to animate the 3D models.

Importing and playing animations of an animated 3D model

To import an animated 3D model, you have to use the BABYLON.SceneLoader class for the static 3D models (Chapter 3, *Create, Load, and Draw 3D Objects on the Screen*) to import an animated 3D model. In fact, the .Load (and .Append) function automatically loads the animated3D models with the associated skeletons (hierarchy of nodes) with the difference that the `.ImportMesh` function's callback provides the loaded meshes, particle systems, and skeletons, as follows:

```
(meshes: AbstractMesh [], particleSystems: ParticleSystem[], skeletons:
Skeleton[]) => void;
```

Concretely, as the animated nodes are the skeletons' bones, the target of the `.beginAnimation` function is only the skeleton associated with your animated 3D model and not the node itself, as follows:

```
// myAnimated3DModel is a BABYLON.Mesh;
var skeleton = myAnimated3DModel.skeleton; // get the skeleton
scene.beginAnimation(
  skeleton, // Target to animate
  0, // The start frame
  150, // The end frame
  true, // Loop ?
  1.0, // Speed ratio
  () => { // Animation end callback
    console.log("Animation of skeleton finished!");
  }
);
```

Let's start an example (available in the example files) using the `.ImportMesh` function, as shown in the following snippet:

```
// Import an animated 3D model
BABYLON.SceneLoader.ImportMesh(
  "", // Names of the specific
  "./", // The root URL
  "dude.babylon", // The name of the scene containing the meshes
  scene, // The scene where to add the meshes
  (meshes, particleSystems, skeletons) => { // callback success
    // Simply start the animations of the skeleton associated
    // To the mesh
    this._scene.beginAnimation(skeletons[0], 0, 150, true, 1.0);
  }
);
```

 Note: An animated 3D model can contain multiple meshes. This is the reason the `ImportMesh` function can return an array of multiple meshes and only one skeleton in the array of skeletons.

The result (the man is walking and the animation played from frame 0 to 150) is as shown in the following image:

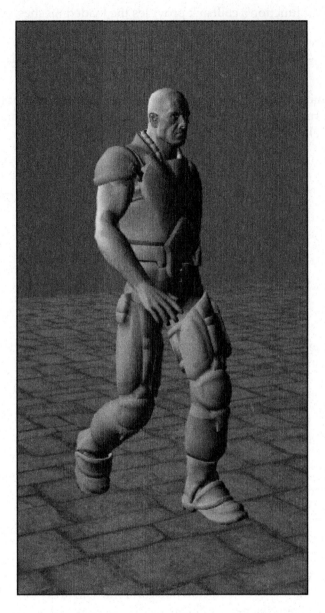

Using the `.Load` function, the method is pretty different. As the success callback provides only the loaded scene, you'll have to find the skeletons stored in the scene. To do this, simple use the `.getSkeletonByName` function on the scene, as follows:

```
BABYLON.SceneLoader.Append(
```

```
"./", // The root url
"dude.babylon", // The name of the scene
scene, // The scene where to append
(scene) => { // The success callback
  // Get the skeleton
  var skeleton = this._scene.getSkeletonByName("Skeleton0");
  // Simply animate the skeleton
  scene.beginAnimation(skeleton, 0, 150, true, 1.0);
}
);
```

The result with the dude.babylon scene using the .Load function is as shown in the following image:

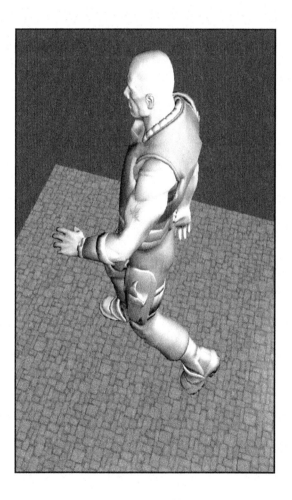

Summary

Creating animations using Babylon.js can really make your scenes more alive. As you can see, these features are also pretty simple to use, following the principle of Babylon.js: the KISS principle (Keep It Simple, Stupid).

Now, at the end of this book, you are ready to work with the artists and combine all the learned features of Babylon.js. Using post-processes, manage and customize materials, create and manage animations, load scenes, manage actions, and so on!

To go further, you can have a look at the new features (recently released) such as the materials library (a library of specific easy-to-use materials like the standard material, such as water, terrain material, PBR, lava, and so on!). One of the new features should be the procedural textures automatically handled by Babylon.js such as fire, ground, grass, and so on. Also, to go further, you can take a look at the particle systems and shadows generator for specific projects that need to create some smoke or fire, and more beautiful (but more expansive) scenes.

Have fun with Babylon.js!

Index

V

value condition 117, 119
variance shadow maps (VSM) 47

vertex shader 56, 57
volumetric light scattering (VLS)
  about 140
  customizing 144

All About Packt

Thank you for buying Babylon.js Essentials

About Packt Publishing

Packt, pronounced 'packed', published its first book, *Mastering phpMyAdmin for Effective MySQL Management* , in April 2004, and subsequently continued to specialize in publishing highly focused books on specific technologies and solutions.

Our books and publications share the experiences of your fellow IT professionals in adapting and customizing today's systems, applications, and frameworks. Our solution-based books give you the knowledge and power to customize the software and technologies you're using to get the job done. Packt books are more specific and less general than the IT books you have seen in the past. Our unique business model allows us to bring you more focused information, giving you more of what you need to know, and less of what you don't.

Packt is a modern yet unique publishing company that focuses on producing quality, cutting-edge books for communities of developers, administrators, and newbies alike. For more information, please visit our website at www.packtpub.com.

About Packt Open Source

In 2010, Packt launched two new brands, Packt Open Source and Packt Enterprise, in order to continue its focus on specialization. This book is part of the Packt Open Source brand, home to books published on software built around open source licenses, and offering information to anybody from advanced developers to budding web designers. The Open Source brand also runs Packt's Open Source Royalty Scheme, by which Packt gives a royalty to each open source project about whose software a book is sold.

Writing for Packt

We welcome all inquiries from people who are interested in authoring. Book proposals should be sent to author@packtpub.com. If your book idea is still at an early stage and you would like to discuss it first before writing a formal book proposal, then please contact us; one of our commissioning editors will get in touch with you.

We're not just looking for published authors; if you have strong technical skills but no writing experience, our experienced editors can help you develop a writing career, or simply get some additional reward for your expertise.

Mastering JavaScript Design Patterns

ISBN: 978-1-78398-798-6   Paperback: 290 pages

Discover how to use JavaScript design patterns to create powerful applications with reliable and maintainable code

- Learn how to use tried and true software design methodologies to enhance your Javascript code.
- Discover robust JavaScript implementations of classic as well as advanced design patterns.
- Packed with easy-to-follow examples that can be used to create reusable code and extensible designs.

JavaScript and JSON Essentials

ISBN: 978-1-78328-603-4   Paperback: 120 pages

Successfully build advanced JSON-fueled web applications with this practical, hands-on guide

- Deploy JSON across various domains.
- Facilitate metadata storage with JSON.
- Build a practical data-driven web application with JSON.

	**Multiplayer Game Development with HTML5** ISBN: 978-1-78528-310-9 Paperback: 180 pages Build fully-featured, highly interactive multiplayer games with HTML5. • Design, develop, manage, debug, and release your multiplayer web-based HTML5 games. • Allow players to go head to head against each other, or collaborate together in the same game world. • A progressive, hands-on guide that builds on an existing single-player game, and adds more networking capabilities at each of the iterations.
	**JavaScript Promises Essentials** ISBN: 978-1-78398-564-7 Paperback: 90 pages Build fully functional web applications using Promises, the new standard in JavaScript • Integrate JavaScript Promises into your application by mastering the key concepts of the Promises API. • Replace complex nested callbacks in JavaScript with the more intuitive chained Promises. • Acquire the knowledge needed to start working with JavaScript Promises immediately.

Please check **www.PacktPub.com** for information on our titles

CPSIA information can be obtained at www.ICGtesting.com
Printed in the USA
BVOW09s1403140316

440260BV00021B/277/P